YOUR HEALTH

YOUR HEALTH

A PRACTICAL PLAN ACCORDING TO GOD'S WORD

RICK THOMAS

YOUR HEALTH:
A Practical Plan According to God's Word

ISBN 978-1-966741-13-8

Rick Thomas

Edited by Sheron Wallace

Life Over Coffee
8595 Pelham Rd Ste 400 #406,
Greenville, SC 29615
LifeOverCoffee.com

Dedication

To Rose
I'll never forget the night you asked me about smoking
cigarettes.

Warning

We do not provide medical advice. Please consult your trusted medical community for their perspectives, advice, and recommended paths forward before you take any action that affects or alters your health.

For additional resources, visit
lifeovercoffee.com

Table of Contents

Preface

Your health isn't just about what you eat or the size you wear. Most people approach health with a narrow focus on diet, weight, or appearance, but true health is much deeper than that. In this book, I will challenge you to think of health holistically—caring for your body and soul from the inside out.

Starting with the common temptations that often derail us (Introduction), I provide practical guidance on building habits that nourish both body and soul (Chapter 1). I then help you learn how to manage thoughts that might derail your journey, reinforcing that health isn't just about food choices but also about your entire being.

In Chapters 3 through 8, we'll delve into specific topics, such as nutrition, sleep, and addictive behaviors, with insights that apply to sound healthy choices. Chapter 6 highlights an often-overlooked factor: how others' actions impact our well-being, underscoring the crucial role of relational harmony in our health journey. Supportive relationships can significantly enhance your health, while toxic ones can complicate it.

Because sound health is as spiritual as it is physical, this book wouldn't be complete without focusing on prayer and rest. Spiritual soundness grounds and sustains every aspect of our well-being. I hope this book will lead to lasting physical and spiritual transformation. After all, enduring health begins with the heart; without that core change, any external transformation won't last.

Rick

Introduction

The New Testament provides three categories to help people think about and work through their temptations. Resolving debilitating short-term and life-long habits does not always happen the same way for all people. Not only are there different strokes for different folks, but there can be different strokes for each person depending on how a specific temptation causes them to stumble or stall. These three ways to overcome temptation and sin can overlap and intersect as you work through a recurring problem. Let's take a look at each one.

Amputation

> And if your right hand causes you to sin, cut it off and throw it away. For it is better that you lose one of your members than that your whole body go into hell.
>
> (Matthew 5:30)

In this passage, Jesus is teaching us that if your eye sins against you, then you should pluck it out, or if your hand offends you, then you should cut it off and throw it away. He uses hyperbolic language that you should not take literally, as it would be profoundly tragic for anyone to make His words a literal mandate for mutilation. He uses "cut-off language" to show the severity of our habituations and how to think about and respond to sin patterns and problems. Sometimes, you should cut off things that tempt you to sin (2 Timothy 2:22). We're talking about behavioral modification. What do you need to cut out of your life?

- Should you say "no" to food?
- Should you resist the temptation to shop?
- Should you turn off the television?
- Should you walk away from social media?
- Should you stop flirting with the opposite sex?
- Should you get up on time and go to bed on time?
- Should you put restrictions on your computer?

External habits and behaviors are in view in the language of Jesus. The cutting-off method can sometimes accomplish the instantaneous cessation of sin, though that is not always the case. In other situations, the battle is more intense and internal, where cutting the sin out of your life does not end the temptation. There is more work to do in the heart.

However, in a counterintuitive way, the ongoing temptation can be a measure of God's kindness to you. The Lord may allow struggles in your life to help you draw closer to Him (2 Corinthians 1:8-9; 12:7-10). Perhaps reading the story of Joseph beginning in Genesis 37 would reveal how the Lord uses sin sinlessly to mature us in the faith. Regardless, we should consider the grace of amputation and how behavioral modification could be a great start to removing sin from our lives.

Mortification

For if you live according to the flesh you will die, but if by the Spirit you put to death the deeds of the body, you will live.

(Romans 8:13)

In Romans, Paul introduces another idea for overcoming sin problems, which speaks more to our hearts. He asks us to mortify the deeds of the body. In our modern Bible, it may read "to make dead" or "to put to death." Mortification is different from cutting off behaviorally. Mortification suggests you may need another method to overcome sin—something deeper. Sometimes, you amputate the problem from your life, and other times, you mortify it. In some situations, you may do both. The mortification of sin reduces the vitality of something until it dies. It takes its strength away. I have illustrated this by using the "common cold" analogy.

I can wipe my child's nose (amputation), and it will take away the manifestation of the problem while bringing external help, albeit limited. These behavioral practices will not address the root issue. The problem is deeper than external solutions. The disease is in the body. There needs to be an internal solution. Therefore, I give our child medicine that I trust will render dead the disease that is internally defiling her. I can tell our child to stop coughing, which would probably exasperate her. She cannot quit no matter how much fussing I do; it will take time. The mortification of sin is a matter of the heart. Here is a list of some of these types of sins:

- Lust for food.
- Bitterness toward someone who wronged you.
- Wrongly motivated by guilt.
- Afraid of what others think about you.
- Worry about making a poor decision.
- Regretting a wrong choice from the past.
- Anxious about how God views you.

Limitation

> Therefore, since we are surrounded by so great a
> cloud of witnesses, let us also lay aside every weight,
> and sin which clings so closely, and let us run with
> endurance the race that is set before us.
>
> (Hebrews 12:1)

The Hebrew writer teaches us to lay aside any weight hindering us. He is not saying that a hindrance is a sin; it does not have to be a sin, but it can be a negative influence—something slowing us down. Sometimes, non-sin things can be sinful to someone, which is why you limit the practice of or participation in those activities. You may not be able to make a biblical case for it being a sin for all of your friends, but you must be self-aware and honest about how temptation grabs your heart, circumventing putting Christ on display in the most effective ways in your life. There are many illustrations of non-sin things that can be sinful to a unique individual. Television, technology, shopping, alcohol, friends, social media, and money are a few examples of non-sin things that can work against us, even to the point of our hearts leading us into sin.

It is important to have a comprehensive understanding of our temptations, weaknesses, and sin patterns so we can be vigilant in refraining from the things that keep the Lord's glory from being reflected in our lives. We must think realistically about how and why we sin and the biblically informed methods that enable us to conquer the things that want to defeat us. Our efforts happen under, in, through, and by the empowering favor of God. We can defeat the enemy's enticements and keep from his entanglements as we respond to the Lord's practical mercy in our lives.

Call to Action

1. What are your struggles?
2. How do you fight the battle against sin?
3. Do you have clear sin categories? Do you call what you do sin when it is sinful, or do you round the corners of your sin by relabeling, redefining, or other minimizing tactics?
4. Have you permitted your friends to speak into your life?
5. Have you shared with them how you sin and how you are tempted to sin?
6. What does this quote mean to you? "The gospelized person is free. He has nothing to hide, nothing to protect, and nothing to fear. He radically battles sin in the context of a community of friends."

1

Doing Without Thinking

Doing things without thinking is one of God's greatest favors to us. It's a communicable attribute. God has given us the ability to respond as sentient creatures to the smaller things of life so we can spend our time thinking about the vital things of life. Great habits—developed over time—free us to image God more effectively because these habituations enable us to focus on what is essential for spreading God's fame.

Let's say that you have just arrived at work. Before you get out of the car, you reflect on the drive. You don't remember it. The daily commute is a habit. You've made that trip so many times that your mind released you from paying attention to the commute. I'm talking about kinesthetic memory. It's the ability to do something without full cognitive awareness. Some people call it muscle memory. I call it habits. Regardless of how you label it, the Lord gave us this means of grace to help us function at maximum capacity. There are many examples of good habituations.

- You ride a bicycle without looking at the pedals. If your feet slip off, you automatically, without looking, put them back on the pedals.

- You type while looking at the computer screen, paying no attention to where your fingers land on the keypad.
- You get out of bed each day, giving no thought to going from lying down to walking upright.

It would blow our minds to think about the number of things we do each minute of the day that require no literal thoughts. The Lord did an amazing job creating us. Think again about your drive to work.

- You drive while staying alert to the other drivers.
- You listen to my podcast while pressing the brake pedal.
- You daydream while watching for the light to change and listening to my podcast.
- You observe a dancing lady with a big sign in front of the pawn shop while feeling your phone vibrate as you navigate a busy intersection.
- You review your shopping list after work to ensure you don't miss anything. You want a happy spouse.

I praise you, for I am fearfully and wonderfully made. Wonderful are your works; my soul knows it very well.

(Psalm 139:14)

The upside to habits is that you can't live without them. There is too much going on to be a single-tasking human. Nobody knows this better than a mom with young children. She is not allowed to do one thing at a time. If she could not develop good habits, she would go crazy, literally. Carrying a newborn in her arms and making hot tea while talking to her three-year-old is an art. Oh, and the phone is blasting a tune from her husband, "Another one bites the dust." She responds instinctively, without thinking.

The Downside

Then there is sin, humanity's common adversary. The nature of sin implies that habits are not always good for us. Sometimes, habits take us to destructive places in our lives and relationships. The downside to sinful habits is that we must guard our minds by giving reflective thought to the bad things we do without thinking. More than likely, you do those things because of well-developed patterns. Like the drive to work, you can get in a relational scrape with a friend in a nanosecond, not realizing how you got there because you have developed bad habits. Repentance is never complete until you change those habits.

Too often, a person will sin, confess their sin, and ask for forgiveness, but never change the habits that caused the sin (Ephesians 4:22-24). Repentance means we have changed our old way to a new way that looks like Jesus. We must do more than acknowledge what we did wrong. We must do more than ask the offended for forgiveness. If sin is a pattern in our lives, we must take our souls to task and unpack the things that have dulled our minds and captured our hearts, keeping us doing what we did. Sinful habit patterns are our call to think about how we came to the place of mentally disengaged behavior.

The Overeating Habit

This perspective is why I write about the motivations of the heart that lead us to do the things we do. If we eat too much, weigh too much, or have other sinful practices, we must deal with the underlying issues of the heart while interacting—secondarily—with the behaviors. So, lets delve more into our behaviors and how our habits give shape to them. If you're going to change, you must dig deep to get at the heart-motivated causes of your habits. I'm using overeating to illustrate, but you can apply these ideas to any bad behavior. Anger, porn, oversleeping, and smoking are four common bad practices that tempt people to indulge themselves. I want you to substitute whatever your bad habit is with my illustration of overeating.

Mable is overweight. She knows it but does not know what to do about it. Mable read my thoughts on overeating and seems to be getting a handle on her anxiousness and worry patterns—the heart issues that feed her desire to eat too much. She also understands her craving for comfort and control, which are born out of a spirit of fear. But Mable continues to eat more than she should. She has not addressed those un-perceived thoughts that trigger her to go for food. Mable is like a sleepwalker. She moves about her home, nibbling-to-scarfing, without realizing what she is doing. Though she may be tacitly aware, she doesn't fully understand it. Her habits are part of her psyche—her soul: the non-organic part of her. Because all habits work this way, she cannot change until she "wakes up" and realizes what she does to herself while in this soul sleep.

Counseling the Habituated

Habits can be what we do every day and can also be what we do seasonally. Seasonal habituation could be just as detrimental—holidays, birthdays, or anniversaries. For many of our brothers and sisters, the Christmas holiday is the stimulus for bad habits. They eat too much because of the ubiquity of food. For others, it's their first season without someone, so they indulge themselves. These bad habits can become the everyday makeup of a person's life. It is who they are. Perhaps you know someone like this and are not surprised by their actions. Over time, you accept them as they are without helping them overcome their caught-ness (Galatians 6:1-2). There are three primary reasons for not being a better friend:

- You are afraid to address the caught person.
- You don't know how to talk to the caught person.
- You don't realize the person is trapped.

If you want to help them, you must look for their trigger points when addressing their habituated patterns (everyday lifestyle habits). Trigger points are what happens to a person that motivates them to develop their habit. Here are a few examples:

- **EXAMPLE #1:** A guy trained himself to look at porn every time his wife leaves home. After she leaves, something inside him begins to burn. It is like the world's largest magnet pulling him to his computer screen.
- **EXAMPLE #2:** A lady trained herself to sleep when things get tough. When life circumstances become challenging, she escapes through sleeping. After a decade of avoiding conflict, she is like a drug addict taking a drug-induced trip. She sleeps through life, hoping things will change.
- **EXAMPLE #3:** The angry spouse's wife trained herself to eat in response to her husband's displeasure. She felt unsafe and wanted comfort. Her God-given desire for love was soured, so she turned to sweets. What she meant for good became an evil means of solace.
- **EXAMPLE #4:** A teen lives in a dysfunctional home. His parents always bicker with each other, and he has no way to leave. Video gaming has become his go-to habit. Now, he's addicted; his grades are falling.

All four people wrongly responded to the trigger points in their lives. At one time, they probably could have walked away from their negative responses to sin, but now they can't. They used to be in control, but now their habits control them. Their sinful reactions to the sinfulness in their world are as unnoticed as the lady who does not remember her morning drive to work. She arrives and reflects on the journey, amazed she made it without killing someone. The overeater finishes the ice cream and reflects on what she did. Her sadness motivates her to eat more—another bad habit.

Practical Tips

Brothers, if anyone is caught in any transgression, you who are spiritual should restore him in a spirit of gentleness. Keep watch on yourself, lest you too be tempted. Bear one another's burdens, and so fulfill the law of Christ. For if anyone thinks he is something, when he is nothing, he deceives himself.
(Galatians 6:1-3)

The first thing to do for the habituated person is to talk with them about their habituation. Draw attention to what is going on in their lives. Help them see the benefits and liabilities of habits. They must understand how the Lord gave them habits to survive and how the devil twisted the Lord's kindness to destroy them (John 10:10). As they gain clarity, they begin unpacking the process that habituated them. Start with the trigger points—the things they do when temptation comes. Discover the sinful stimulus that motivates them to respond to problems with bad practices. Discern their caught-ness. If this is the beginning stage of bad habits, it won't be hard to stem the tide. However, if this has been a habituation for many years, your work will be challenging. Walk through all the triggers. There may be more than one, especially if they have developed a pattern of wrong responses to adverse circumstances.

Typically, there may be only one trigger in the beginning— the angry husband. In this scenario, the wife began to eat after each time he railed at her. Overeating became her habit. With no one challenging her response to his sin, she began to eat when any conflict, difficulty, or unnerving situation came into her life. Now, she is controlled and managed by many triggers. You want to spend time with her to talk about all the negative situations in her life and how she habitually responds. She is genuinely caught in her sin, though the original cause was not her fault. Make sure this is clear to her. She is the sinning victim—a person who sins in response to being sinned against. She needs to cultivate the awareness to recognize what is happening to her and how she responds to her husband's actions.

This process takes much prayer. She must regularly engage the Spirit, asking Him to illuminate her mind to what is happening in these moments. It would be great if she learned the habits of pre-praying, praying at the moment, and post-praying. These are cultivated attitudes and behaviors of prayer before the temptation comes, during the temptation, and after it leaves. Whether she fails or not, she must become a prayer warrior to break this habitation. Passive obedience is not enough. She must actively engage God. Teach her other habits, too. For the overeater, she can make healthy selections like carrots, apples, oranges, or celery. She does not have to stop eating but must eat more nutritiously. Finally, teach her about the grace of God that works in her failures because she will fail. Encourage her. Let her know it's okay to fail. She is not going for unbroken, idealized perfection; she is going for gradual transformation. She will never be perfect. She wants to create a pattern of positive habits while factoring in the possibility of episodic failures.

Call to Action

When helping the habituated, ensure they agree to allow you to speak into their lives. Changing years of bad habits will take much work, and they cannot do it alone. Make plans to connect with them occasionally. As they progress, you may be able to address the other issues connected to the bad situation in their lives. It would be great if they stopped tormenting themselves, but for now, you need to stabilize them by helping them break the bad habits.

1. What are the upsides of habits? Name a few of yours.
2. What are the downsides of habits? Name a few of yours.
3. How did you develop good habits, and how did you develop bad habits?
4. What do you need to do to change your bad habits? What is your specific and practical plan to change?

2

Idol Swapping

All external, behavioral idols have the same insidious root cause—unbelief, or its synonym, self-reliance. The self-reliant spirit is not trusting God. If you don't deal with this universal heart problem, you could easily stop one sin while jumping to a different idol. Have you ever played "whack-a-mole" at an amusement center? It's one of those games where plastic moles randomly pop up while you try to whack them with a rubber mallet before they retreat into their holes. You never know when or where one will pop up. As soon as you knock one down, another one jumps up.

The Idol Swapper

It's a picture of our hearts. When you beat down one idol, another one pops up to take its place. John Calvin supposedly said that our hearts are like idol factories. My friend, Biff, would agree. He had a secret porn addiction for nearly three decades. Through a series of providential circumstances, his sin was found out by his boss. Biff was humbled by being exposed, and he repented from the addiction. Mercifully, his boss decided not to fire him. He appealed to Biff to let his wife and pastor know about his porn problem. Biff followed through with his request.

After speaking with his pastor, Biff sought counseling, which he attended bi-weekly. During the counseling, Biff continued to show evidence of repentance. He put safety software on his computer and other devices. He gave his wife all his passwords and access to his tech toys. He joined a men's group at his church. Biff was hitting all the right buttons, and his addiction began to wane. After about six weeks of counseling, Biff shared how he had gained weight. His counselor had already observed this but did not bring it to Biff's attention.

The Idol Factory

Biff's admission opened a door for the counselor to have a more in-depth conversation about matters of the heart and self-reliance. The counselor began by encouraging him about his behavioral changes (Matthew 5:29-30) but noted that his repentance was incomplete. With great care and gentle accountability, Biff was freeing himself from the porn addiction. The more in-depth problem was not addressing the root cause of the addiction—a man not fully trusting God, choosing to rely on himself instead. His counselor had been hoping to get into this discussion because he knew if Biff did not deal with self-reliance, he would do one of two things:

- He would revert to his porn addiction.
- He would jump to another addiction: food.

In Biff's case, he stopped porn and started eating too much. He had essentially swapped his original idol for food. Biff did not understand how his self-reliance still affected him. External idols like porn, eating too much, alcohol, watching too much TV, overspending, or lack of exercise can have the same insidious root cause. They can be God-substitutes designed to relieve a person who struggles with relying on God. This attitude of the heart is one reason we should not condemn our friends who are stuck in sins, unlike ours. The lady who sinfully seeks comfort through overspending or overeating can be ruled by a similar heart of unbelief like Biff. Though our outer lives can be vastly different and somewhat unique in what we enjoy, we come from the same "Adamic cloth" (Romans 5:12). Trusting God moment by moment is a daily challenge.

> The heart is deceitful above all things, and desperately sick; who can understand it?
>
> (Jeremiah 17:9)

At the core of Biff's heart, he had not changed. He merely swapped his idol of choice from one addiction to the next. If not for the weight gain, it could have been possible never to realize his idol-swapping. While you don't want to micromanage a person, you want to be discerning and loving enough to regard the heart's deceptions. The goal is not to condemn or overly scrutinize anyone but to serve and love them through wise soul care. God has given us a spirit of discernment, and we should use this Spirit's gifts for His glory and the good of others. We should think deeper than how our world thinks (John 2:24-25). We should make sound biblical assessments that take our care of people to greater depths. Understanding biblical psychology—the study of the soul—permits Christians to do what no other demographic can (Genesis 2:7; 2 Timothy 3:16-17). We can address the fruit (porn) and the root of our problems (unbelief).

Beyond the Fruit

Idol swapping should be a biblical assumption when counseling someone habituated in long-term sin patterns (Galatians 6:1). Putting away a former manner of life (Ephesians 4:22) that has characterized a person for 30 years cannot come without a fight (1 Peter 5:8). Sin is chaos of the soul. It takes time to restore order to a person who has been habituated to a pattern of thinking and behaving for most of their life. This challenge gives us an advantage in soul care. We understand how habituation in external sin is more than what a person can see. Though you want to applaud Biff for cutting the original addiction out of his life (Matthew 5:30), you want to ensure he has sufficiently put to death the heart of sin that fed his first addiction—his functional atheism, an unwillingness to fully trust God (Romans 8:13).

Fruit trees begin the growth process beneath the soil. Long before the fruit manifests, there is a lot of activity beyond the gaze of the human eye. This illustration depicts how sin works. Cutting down a tree does not kill the tree. There is still life silently forming in the root system, mostly undisturbed. You could unwisely assume the tree is dead. It's only a season or two later when you learn that you did not complete the job. Biff had been doing an excellent job cutting the rotten fruit out of his life and trimming back a few limbs. According to many of his friends, he was not the same guy; he was noticeably different, and a spiritual revival was occurring. From a cursory perspective, he appeared to be okay, but if you spent time with him, you would notice how some things under the surface of his life had not changed.

Idol of Self-reliance

Though we can tweak our physical selves into something that may resemble Jesus, we can't as easily do the same for the hidden man of the heart. This kind of internal change is a gift from the Lord (2 Timothy 2:25). It's a cooperative effort: God grants repentance, and we obediently respond to His kindness. Biff had not honestly dealt with his long-term underlying unbelief that motivated him to rely on himself. I'm not suggesting he was blatantly deceitful or not a believer. He did not know what was wrong with him. He was like many Christians who have not been discipled to where they can shepherd their hearts. Biff was doing what he knew to do—rely on himself, which led to the porn problem. He knew the porn was wrong, so he stopped. His problem was he did not know what else was wrong with him—what was the cause that created the temptation to porn.

He had a worship disorder of the heart—a self-reliant spirit that lived in defiance of God. Biff was an unbelieving believer; instead of trusting God, he preferred to operate his world according to the outcomes he determined. When you looked inside his heart, you saw the idols that fed his self-reliant spirit—the same idols for all self-reliant people. This deeper looked revealed how the porn problem was a respite for a man trying to run his world according to his dreams. When you attempt to run your life according to your plans, you will grow weary, which is the predicate for an escape. Porn was Biff's escape that gave him temporary relief from the audacious task of relying on himself. Here are the four specific idols that fed his self-reliance, propelling him to create an addictive escape.

Idol of Control

The first thing you see in Biff's heart—that fuels his self-reliance—is the idol of control. The self-reliant person has to be in control, the only way to manage his self-reliance. Biff is what the world calls a "Type A" personality, not a compliment as much as it is a liability to the biblically uncalibrated heart. Biff did not fully trust the Lord, which is why control was so critical for him. He had to maintain control of his world, an impossible task. For Biff, this impossibility is where his escape comes into play. The overworked soul, who refuses to rely on God, needs an occasional escape. It's the "you need a break today" syndrome. Porn became a quickie pit stop for Biff to escape from the pressures of running his world without God.

Idol of Comfort

Looking farther into his idol factory, you would observe the idol of comfort. If you reject God as your source of strength, choosing to rely on yourself, you must figure out how to run your universe under your own power. Biff's comfort zone was working within his finite strengths, which made him amazing as long as he could control all things "through Biff who strengthen Biff" (Philippians 2:13). Of course, the pressure was too much, so Biff would escape into porn for relief. You can see how his idols of comfort and control interconnect with each other.

Idol of Fear

As we explore his idol factory further, we find low-level fear operating in his heart. Biff was afraid to trust God. He always had a profound sense of masked fear, which was not perceptible from ground level. People who knew Biff would not categorize him as fearful. This "Type A" man was an insecure man. His low-grade insecurity motivated him to crave comfort—operating within his own strengths. When he found his sweet spot, he maintained absolute control of his world. Of course, as I've already noted, it's hard to be a god. You must take breaks from running your universe. Hence his addictive behavior.

Idol of Unbelief

The biggest idol of them all, the one that fed his fears, motivated him to crave comfort and convinced him to seize control of his world, was unbelief. Though Biff was a believer from a salvation perspective, he was not a believer from a sanctification perspective. He had an immature relationship with God. There were many reasons for this.

- His dad was not a great guy, so Biff didn't trust authority figures, and he mapped his experiences over God.
- He grew up in a fear-based, fundamentalist culture. Thus, he assumed he had to perform for the Lord.
- He was uniquely depraved, which is Adam's unbelief.
- He had an unhealthy fear of God—he did not feel secure with the Lord, a product of his legalism.
- He also experienced a few disappointments, which he unwittingly attributed to God.

Though he never walked away from God, his heart drifted from the Lord. Like a man falling asleep on a boat, he awoke miles from where he had gone to sleep. Biff had been in a spiritual slumber for many years. He slowly habituated himself to his addiction, and the hardening of his heart blinded him to where he could not discern his functional atheism (Hebrews 3:7-8). Because of the mercy of the Lord, the scales were removed from his eyes. This divine kindness happened after his boss busted him for his porn addiction. He gained the clarity to stop but still could not see the hidden idolatry of self-reliance in his heart.

Taste and See

As the counselor addressed these idols, Biff began to see the corruptness of his soul and how he had defamed the Lord all these years. He began to learn how to renew his mind (Ephesians 4:23) about the true and living God. He learned about the gospel and how the Lord went to death to rescue him from hell. In time, Biff became a believing believer. He learned the Lord is not like his dad and that true religion is not fear-based. He also knew that even though God was not safe, He was good and would challenge him but never harm him (Hebrews 12:6). A distaste began to form in Biff's heart for these cravings for comfort and control. He was no longer managed by fear. He was learning to do "all things through Christ who strengthen him" (Philippians 4:13).

Biff began to put his self-reliance to death by trusting God in ways he had not in the past. His most significant tests came when the stress and busyness of life tempted him to find refuge through his old habits. In the past, he would find escapes through addictions. Today, he seeks refuge through prayer, Bible reading, and honest conversations with his wife and friends. The Lord has given him a servant's heart. Instead of selfishly heaping pleasure on himself, he has a passion for spreading the love of Christ to others by serving them in tangible ways. His transformation became complete. He not only stopped the external manifestation of idolatry that got him into trouble, but he defeated the idols of his heart, which fed those behaviors.

Call to Action

1. How about you? Are you finding refuge in other things?
2. Is there something about the Lord that has yet to be worked out in your heart to the point where He is not your first and most satisfying choice?
3. Discuss the concept of idol-swapping with a friend. Perhaps you can share an experience where you swapped idols and how the Lord brought it to light. Maybe it will open the door for a conversation with your friend who might be struggling like Biff.

3

Let's Talk Weight Loss

Weight loss is one of the most sensitive subjects we can discuss today. Image-type discussions are more personal than the things we cannot observe about each other. Some folks are so opposed to talking about it that they have redefined what overweight and obesity are; we prefer to think of ourselves as body-positive regardless of how unhealthy we might be or what comorbidities we're accumulating. Thankfully, the Bible cuts through the confusion with a clarity that helps us change into Christlike vessels, inside and out.

The Battle of the Bulge

There are seasons in our lives when the temptations to resist self-control and discipline are strong. The holidays, personal and relational challenges, and sheltering in place come to mind. Then, we come to our senses, start a new diet, and jump in the gym as we take our pledges to fight the battle of the bulge. These resolutions are commonplace because many people struggle with their weight. Self-awareness does not have to be bad news. It could be the motivation you need to take action. We want to be in tune with the things we want to change. Losing weight and taking better care of our bodies is an excellent idea, as well as a biblical one, so let's go ahead and get two familiar verses out of the way since you're anticipating them.

> Or do you not know that your body is a temple of the Holy Spirit within you, whom you have from God? You are not your own, for you were bought with a price. So glorify God in your body.
> (1 Corinthians 6:19-20)

> So, whether you eat or drink, or whatever you do, do all to the glory of God.
> (1 Corinthians 10:31)

These verses are great, and I am sure they are familiar to you. Perhaps you have read them many times but are still battling the bulge. May I be honest? I struggle with weight gain, too. Sometimes, the Word of God comes across as a book of black letters on white pages—especially if we do not approach the Bible biblically. It's vital to know that the words in the Bible are not magical, like waving a wand. There is power, but that power does not work passively, randomly, or arbitrarily. The power of the Word works in proportion to our proper engagement with those Words while actively praying, authentically seeking, humbly expecting, practically applying, and transparently living in the context of a biblical community.

Thinking Biblically

If we think wrongly about the change process, we will become disappointed when our weight does not move the needle in the right direction. The issue here is not an under-appreciation of the Word of God as it is a lack of knowing what the change process requires. It is similar to teaching a child to do right, but he does not follow through with your guidance because he needs to learn how. The words appear to fall on deaf ears. God's Word can fall on deaf ears, too (Hebrews 5:11-14). Therefore, we must,

1. Respond to the Word of God.
2. Engage the Spirit of God.
3. Actively appropriate the grace of God.
4. Practically seek the community of God.

We can make great strides in heart and body alterations as we do these things. So, with these disciplines in mind, consider how to bring the Word of God to bear on being overweight. Let's begin with two fundamental questions:

- How do you link the Bible to addictions?
- Specifically, how do you practically connect the Word to overeating?

Below the Surface

I love those questions because making Bible connections to our lives is imperative. More specifically, I'm speaking of what the Bible teaches us about connecting the gospel to our sanctification. Losing weight makes the gospel question an important one. Therefore, you ask, "What does the gospel have to do with eating too much?" There are two ways to think about and apply the gospel to the problem of overeating:

- Overeating is not the real problem but a symptom of a deeper problem, which the gospel addresses.
- Our bodies do not belong to ourselves; God purchased us with the gospel.

One of the advantages of Christian discipleship over secular self-help is that the Christian discipler does not stop with behavioral modification. While we must change our behaviors—eating poorly or too much—we know true change won't happen until we address the source of the problem. For example, Jesus tied the tongue—the words we use (symptom)—to the heart—who we are (core problem)— in Luke 6:45. We find a connection between the words we use and our hearts. Similarly, being overweight is not an external problem with no relationship to our inner selves— who we are at the core of our being. We are not biblically allowed to say, "I'm fat," and act as though our external condition disconnects from the internal state of our hearts. Here is a shortlist of potential soul problems a Christian discipler wants to explore with a person who is overweight:

Anxiety	Fear	Self-reliance
Performance	Sadness	Arrogance
Lack Self-control	Unbelief	Self-righteous
Frustration	Comfort	Anger
Slothful/lazy	Folly/impulsive	Disappointment
Jealousy	Regret	Envy
Resentment	Hopelessness	Apathy

Purchased by the Gospel

Are any of these characteristics part of who you are? If so, there is a more significant issue besides lack of exercise, overeating, or poor food choices. In most cases with the overweight person, it is a soul problem too. Though there are a few people where overweight and obesity struggles can be an organic problem only, it would be unwise to neglect a fuller exploration of the whole person before settling on organic exclusivity. Can you see how the deeper issues listed will feed the temptation to overeat or not exercise? How aware are you that the gospel speaks specifically to someone struggling with those underlying issues? The gospel brings hope and help to the craving or disappointed heart, and with that kind of internal support, the overweight person eventually experiences external transformation.

- The gospel addresses the source of our problems.
- The gospel does not allow us to do whatever we want.

The gospel teaches how the Lord executed His Son (Isaiah 53:10) on the cross to redeem hopeless and helpless souls (Ephesians 2:8-9). Our souls were the most expensive purchase ever made. However, the gospel goes beyond redeeming us. After the good Lord regenerated us, He began to abide in us, and we in Him (John 15:4). Thus, we can make these four gospel connections:

- I am no longer my own.
- I no longer have the right to do whatever I want to do with my body.
- I am in union with Christ.
- I am an adopted child of the King.

Gospel Motivation

Because of the gospel, we want to make His name great in our lives and among our families, friends, and culture. We want to show the gospel's transformative power to all those desperate for the hope it offers. Suppose we are not rightly and practically affected by the truths of the gospel. If that were true, we would be out of line with the gospel (Galatians 2:14), and we must make our bodies a sacrifice to our Lord (Romans 12:1-2) as vessels that show off the power of the gospel in our lives. The more sobering fact we must deal with is the temptation to suppress the gospel through our lifestyles (Romans 1:18).

Altering the truth is more than an overweight issue. I am talking about our affection for Christ. The power of the gospel bought all of us, body and soul. Therefore, we need to learn how to practically live out all of the inheritance our Father provides for us (1 Peter 1:4). We do not want to live in vain (1 Corinthians 9:27). If your mind is more affected by Christ than food, you are in the perfect position to deal with the core problem with eating too much. Are you ready? The next step is to come to a fuller understanding of how sin operates in your life. I will do this by choosing one of the core heart issues listed above—a lack of self-control.

The Battle of Self-Control

In this instance, part of the overeater's problem is a lack of self-control—a vital aspect of the Spirit's fruit (Galatians 5:22-23). Let's say that self-control is not practically working in Mable's life, so let's examine her struggle. A person with little self-control in one area of life will have self-control problems in other areas, too. For example, a lady who has trouble controlling her eating habits is overweight. In our case study, Mable lacks self-control. But as you talk to her, you realize she lacks self-control in several other areas, like worry, anxiousness, fear, and anger. Sin will never, ever discriminate. Sin seeks to destroy the entire soul, not just part of it. It will corrupt every possible area of our lives, hoping to spread its poison. Rarely will you find a person who struggles with self-control in a monolithic way, like overeating. Here is a possible sin list regarding Mable's weight problems, looking only at self-control. Notice how that one issue snakes its way into other areas of her life.

- She overeats.
- She struggles with time management.

- She has poor work habits.
- She succumbs to fear, worry, and anxiety.
- She spends overspends.
- She binge-watches television.
- She loves hanging out on social media.
- She cares more about herself than others, compounding her isolation and creating an endless loop that amplifies all her problems.

Sadly, There's More

Furthermore, Mable struggles to bring her mind into obedience. For example, she can gossip, be critical, angry, fearful, make uncharitable judgments, rarely think the best of others, and be cynical and self-righteous. Then, other bad habits start showing up on the radar of her heart as she continues in these self-defeating and cyclic patterns, those things that hop a ride on the endless loop that is her orbit. Here are a few more examples:

- She has sporadic downtime with God.
- She lacks discretion, discernment, and wisdom.
- She is lazy when it comes to physical fitness.
- She has poor sleeping habits.

Can you imagine how overwhelming and discouraging it would be when she first perceives a lack of self-control in all these areas? It is like finding the first termite in your home, and after you call the termite man, you realize an infestation of the destructive bugs is consuming the house. Intuitively, we know this is the case with most crucial things in our lives, but knowing something theoretically is a far cry from when those problems "out there somewhere" are destroying us.

The Good News

People typically think the best approach for combating a permeating and pervasive sin like a lack of self-control is to bring every area of their lives back into control at the same time. This approach usually ends with frustration because the overwhelmed person begins to realize resistance is futile. The temptation to despair settles in, begging the question: Is it wise to attack every area simultaneously? I do not think so—at least not always.

KEY IDEA: One of the best ways to practice self-control is to tackle one area of your life that is out of control rather than every area. As you attack a single area, you will learn how to eventually attack all the other areas of your life that are out of control. Here is a list of a few things you will experience as you gain victory in one area:

- You learn practical habits that help you battle against a lack of self-control.
- You learn to pray about the specific sin issue of no self-control.
- You experience growing encouragement as God blesses you with restraint.
- You begin to tell others about what He is doing in your life.
- You are no longer discouraged about this problem and become an encourager to others who lack self-control.
- You gain an understanding of the commitment to learn self-control.
- You appreciate God's grace, enabling you to persevere in self-control.
- You grow in your confidence in the Lord for how He brings all areas of your life into control.
- Your example of living out the gospel by losing weight motivates others to change.

In time, you attack other problem areas because you have learned how to mature in this one area. You can take any problem, e.g., poor sleep habits, gossiping, addictions, working too much, and overspending, and apply these ideas to them and gain victory in your life.

Finally, perhaps the most vital thing you should learn is that transformation on matters like these takes time. You prepare yourself for the long haul while begging God for the perseverance and grace to work it out practically.

Call to Action

We do not provide medical advice. Please consult your trusted medical community for their perspectives, advice, and recommended paths forward before you take any action that alters your health.

1. Are you overweight? Are you obese? Will you be honest about your weight?
2. Will you spend time in prayer, asking the Father to show you the underlying heart issues? Examine your life from a wide-angle perspective, including what is happening in your heart.
3. Create a plan to address each issue one at a time. The pathway ahead of you is challenging, so my strongest appeal is for you to invite someone into your journey and ask them to hold you accountable.
4. Start mapping out a strategy today with measurable goals to start losing weight as you address these core issues of the heart.

4

Three-step Plan

Authentic health initiatives require both body and soul transformation. The secret sauce is a comprehensive approach to losing weight because while behavioral modification might provide quick visual results if we don't change our hearts, those external transformations will revert to our old manner of living. It's like cleaning the outside of the cup but not taking time to clean the inside, which will always leave you in a state of disappointment and possibly despair.

Read the Warning

Because I don't provide medical advice, I always recommend that before any health initiatives, the person checks with their doctor. I say this because what comes next is something that Lucia and I do; it's our plan, not yours. I would not presume to tell you what to do about your health. Each person must seek the Lord, trusted friends, and the medical community to figure out what best suits them in their journey to present their bodies as a testimony to the radicality of the gospel. Additionally, my advice moves beyond the superficial by addressing the heart repentance that must come first. My heart struggles will differ from yours. Most health-related resources that folks rave about are the ones that suggest diets, tips, tricks, best practices, smart food choices, and habit changes. I'm not knocking those things because they do help, but you rarely see programs that discuss the underlying causes of why the person was unhealthy or overweight in the first place.

I'm speaking of repentance, that unspoken non sequitur that we do not usually connect to the deeper and even more challenging struggles of the soul. Of course, throw in the fact that health-related problems are too personal. Body problems fit better in the pantheon of unmentionables like religion and politics, things we don't discuss in polite society, even though we know that the formerly cherished polite society left the station a few decades ago. Regardless, too many of us still don't want to talk about what is wrong with us. My hesitancy about weight loss, healthy eating, and exercise is because I don't want to share my sin list with you—the underlying matters of the heart that create my more oversized, more visible issues. Though I want to live a life of integrity with you and before the Lord, drawing back and hiding parts of my life from the community is a source of temptation. The irony, as well as the deception, is that I can't conceal my physicality from anyone.

But when he came to himself...

(Luke 15:17)

Our Step-By-Step Plan

A few years ago, Lucia and I began a process of repenting of the poor fitness patterns in our lives by sculpting out a practical and workable plan for objective, measurable transformation. The first step in our plan was the most demanding and challenging of the three stages; it was a not-so-simple process to submit our lives to the Lord while holding each other accountable. Here is what we did.

STEP #1: Repentance will determine the quality of your health. You will only reach your goals if you get this first step right. Genuine repentance is not primarily about a plan but about our hearts. There are thousands of weight loss plans in the marketplace. The cultural gurus give us their ideas, but there is only one way to repent: it is a gift from God (2 Timothy 2:24-25). I have tried different plans and programs offered by health advocates. Most worked to some degree, but none hit the target because they were all various forms of behavioral modification. Those plans give you a methodology that focuses on what you can see in the physical world, but they do not target what you cannot see, which is in our hearts—the spiritual person. Though there are practical necessities to losing weight, the more pressing matter is internal transformation.

Put Off the Right Stuff

To put off your old self, which belongs to your former manner of life and is corrupt through deceitful desires, and to be renewed in the spirit of your minds, and to put on the new self, created after the likeness of God in true righteousness and holiness.

(Ephesians 4:22-24)

Putting off bad food and putting on better food does not change what is wrong inside of us, spiritually speaking. Therefore, our goals must be more than looking good on the outside. We must discern and work on what the Lord values. God discerns and treasures our hearts (1 Samuel 16:7; Matthew 23:27). Our primary goal must be more about the Lord's preference for body image instead of cultural pressures. We are on the right path if we start with the heart, which begs the question: repent of what?

Thinking about our souls brings us to the most vital thing when considering the repentance construct: What are the hidden idolatries of our hearts? When I thought about these things, I began writing down those idolatries that tempted me to stay the way I am. Here is my sin list; though it's not exhaustive, it was helpful to bring me to the place where I had to decide if I would live in a self-imposed delusional stupor full of misdirections and rationalizations or honestly cry out to God for help.

Comfort	Anxiety	Fear
Self-reliance	Deceit	Lack Self-control
Worry	Arrogance	Unbelief
Lack Sympathy	Discouragement	Hypocrisy
Blindness	Self-righteousness	Laziness

All Things for Evil

Create in me a clean heart, O God, and renew a right spirit within me.

(Psalm 51:10)

Those hidden idolatries worked together for evil as a sinful constellation that kept me in bondage to poor health. Rather than tackling them all at once, I commenced with one at a time. I chose hypocrisy, as it seemed like a good starting point for the change process. It is hypocritical for me to counsel, disciple, train, or teach other people how to gain victory in any area of their lives when I am not trying to secure victory in a particular area of my life. In my case, poor health choices manifested primarily as overeating, eating the wrong foods, and not exercising.

Hypocrisy is a form of rationalization that stratifies sin by saying, "My sin is not as bad as your sin." Even though the consequences of sin can be different, it is intellectually dishonest to think my sin is of lesser importance to the

Lord (James 2:1). Any sin is enough for Christ to die on the cross. I needed to address my heart sufficiently before engaging the gay guy, the angry guy, the addicted guy, the adulterer, or the victim-centered spouse. I asked the Lord to search my heart, which meant it was time for me to be honest with God, myself, and others (Psalm 139:23-24). Taking the log from my eye first was a better move than intellectually dishonest, spiritualized acrobatics that made me feel superior to others.

Do Not Ignore

I could no longer ignore how my poor health choices were feeding my idolatries, a process that led to another question: "When would I indeed come to the end of myself regarding my health?" No longer could I shuffle my sin inside my head while trying to feel better about myself. It was time to take my soul to task, which meant examining how my heart sins led to behavioral sins. As I work through my list with you, let me explain the connection between heart sins that create personal and relational frustrations.

1. **COMFORT:** Food was a way for me to seek comfort when a better choice would have been to find refuge in the Lord through prayer.
2. **LACK OF SELF-CONTROL:** A lack of resistance to food pointed to my unwillingness to appropriate God's grace regarding the fruit of the Spirit, specifically self-control (Galatians 5:22-23).
3. **SELF-RELIANCE:** "Doing things my way" was not relying on the Lord, which spoke to an underlying attitude toward the Lord: "I can do what I want to do; I do not need you because I am self-sufficient."
4. **FEAR:** Fear is always attached to self-reliance. When things were not going my way, I was afraid. This fear tempted me to seize control of the situation

through self-reliant means.

5. **ANXIETY:** Similar to fear was anxiety. It manifested as stress. When I became anxious, I ran for comfort food.

6. **WORRY:** Worrying is similar to fear and anxiety. It manifests by overthinking a problem rather than trusting the Lord.

7. **DISCOURAGEMENT:** As you can see, my sin constellation is interconnected. Multiple sin patterns intersected and interacted with each other. It is no wonder I became discouraged and sought comfort through eating.

8. **SELF-RIGHTEOUSNESS:** At the core of my idol factory was self-righteousness—a greater than/better than attitude. The Lord prefers the weak, not those so arrogant that they will not humble themselves before Him. Christ came for the broken, not those who pretended to be strong by seeking self-reliant means to keep up pretenses.

9. **ARROGANCE:** See self-righteousness. (I'm in a nasty sin cycle now.)

10. **SPIRITUAL BLINDNESS:** Not biblically responding to my sin list spoke of my spiritual blindness (Hebrews 5:12-14).

11. **LACK OF SYMPATHY:** Jesus faced temptation in every way, which enabled Him to be a sympathizing Savior (Hebrews 4:14-15). The more I engage my struggles, the more I can sympathize with other strugglers, even though our struggles may differ.

12. **LAZINESS:** I am not willing to step up to the plate and do something about my health issues.

13. **DECEIT:** Besides spiritual blindness, I was unwilling to be honest about what I perceived in my heart.

14. **HYPOCRISY:** See my sin list.

15. **UNBELIEF:** The most significant culprit was my weak faith in the Lord.

Post Repentance

Owning these moving parts in my heart motivated me to do something about it. What about you? Though your sin list may differ from mine, you must deal with the ruling motives of your heart because whatever they are, they rule you—for good or evil. If you are willing to take your soul to task by being honest with yourself and God, you can move on to the next step to better health. But first, I want you to answer a few questions.

- Will you do it your way or God's way?
- Will you repent at the heart level of any resident sins, which releases you to make a practical plan for measurable change?
- Will you trust the Lord in word only, or will you trust Him enough to change authentically (James 2:17)?

STEP #2: I told my family what was happening and informed them of my progress. I did not wait for them to ask me. It would help if you held others accountable for holding you accountable. Too often, a person blames friends for not being effective accountability partners. Their complaint may have some truth, but it should not stop you from leading them by being honest, transparent, and forthright about what God is doing in your life and demanding they hold you accountable. Nobody but the Lord will love you how you need to be loved, so you must lead others in loving you well. Be their example. Lead them. Teach them how to take care of you.

Make a Plan

STEP #3: Determine what you will eat. You must insert your personal, doable, practical plan in this step. Your customized plan means you must research and write a proper program. The method you decide to implement will be the core of your program. You and your community must determine what kinds of food you will eat and how much of what food you will eat. Better health happens in a community. Only you, the Lord, your friends, and your medical community can speak to this critical step. The hardest part is what you are doing now—being honest about the true nature of your body and soul.

Finally, to reiterate, we do not provide medical advice. Please consult your trusted medical community for their perspectives, advice, and recommended paths forward before you take any action that alters your health.

Call to Action

1. Will you be honest with the Lord? What would this type of honesty look like for you and among your friends?
2. Will you be honest with yourself? As you do business with the Lord, ask Him to reveal any deceptions or habituations you might have that blind you to what you should see about yourself.
3. Will you be honest with others? Bringing your life to the light of a community is one of the most transforming things you can do.
4. What will be your specific plan?

5

Confession of a Smoker

Rose was a member of my small group. One night, she asked me what I thought about smoking cigarettes. I said, "It's not what's between your fingers that is a problem; it's what is in your heart." At that moment, the Lord did the miraculous. Over the next few months, her heart changed. I was oblivious to all these things. Months later, she shared with me what happened. Please enjoy her confession and praise to God.

Rose's Confession

I did not want to quit smoking. I liked to smoke and felt my smoking wouldn't change my lifespan since God already knows the day we are born and the day we die. I did not think He was up there deducting time off my life for each cigarette I smoked. Of course, I did believe my quality of life would improve if I quit smoking, but that wasn't the selling point for me. I asked Rick about quitting smoking because he kept saying the gospel is the answer to everything. I just couldn't figure out how Jesus dying for my sins and defeating death was an answer to someone trying to give up an addiction like my smoking idol. I asked him to explain this to me, and he did. I do not have the exact words or sketches he drew for me, but I will tell you what struck a chord with me and what I realized since I decided to trust Christ with one of the little things in my life. The most important aspect for me to remember is that I didn't quit smoking; I decided to live in faith, and God did the rest.

Start With the Gospel

For God so loved the world, that he gave his only Son, that whoever believes in him should not perish but have eternal life.

(John 3:16)

If I believe what John said, I should have a response to that verse daily, and that would be my faith expressing itself in my life. Then, I must think of my faith and what that looks like. I go to church meetings, read my Bible, pray, attend care groups, and have fellowship with believers, on and on and on. These disciplines are all me doing things and living in my little Christian box, but where am I growing? I am growing in knowledge and truth, but where is the evidence of my faith manifested in my life? If we are to grow in faith, we need to step out of our boxes; that is where we see the evidence of faith, grace, mercy, and the Holy Spirit dwelling in us and manifesting in our lives. Remember, God always goes before us, and sometimes, He takes us to places outside our daily boxes because He loves us.

God's mysterious and painful work may be the loss of a job, the loss of a loved one, moving to a new state, a troubled teen, facing the fact we have an idol, etc. As far as idols go, it may be that doctor telling you your blood sugar is high, the feeling of being run down all the time, a cough that won't go away. You could have to spend money on new clothes, but your old ones are perfectly fine; they just don't fit anymore.

Suffering is the place that puts feet on our stagnant faith as God places us outside our neat little boxes and asks, "Am I still God when you are out there? Do I still love you when you're out there? Do you still trust in the gospel when you're out there?" At that point, we have to preach the gospel to ourselves and believe in Him again, even though it isn't under our control.

We then must keep walking towards the cross, following Him as He goes before us. Each time He takes us outside our box, and we trust in Him fully, our box gets bigger (our faith increases), and our praise grows as our testimony for Him grows. All the glory belongs to Him! Realizing I had been growing in knowledge and truth for many years by receiving the gospel made me realize God was equipping me for this stepping out of the box, and I was immediately amazed by His kindness. At that point, I had not even decided to give my cigarettes to Christ, but I had to examine my motives for giving them to Him. I would have to trust Him daily and walk closely with Him physically, emotionally, and spiritually. I would have to put all my weight on Him. Our confidence in Him has to be exactly that: our trust in Him!

Crying like an Infant

For me, especially giving smoking over to Him was the hardest part as I sat on my knees, face on the ground in my bathroom for over two hours, crying like an infant, talking with God. My conversation was like this:

> I know you are who you say you are, and I know I can trust you. I know you will take this from me, and I won't have to worry about it, but I have to be the one to give it to you, and this is the part I am struggling with the most. I have to choose between trusting in you and trusting in my idol. To trust in you means I must relinquish my idol to you today by

trusting in you, and then I have to choose to trust in you daily to sustain me.

As I was having this conversation with God, it became apparent by giving God this idol, I was living out the gospel. Therefore, the gospel is the answer to everything. After I had put the burden of my idol on Him, my responsibility of trusting Him daily was light. BAM!! There you go, the gospel once again!! Since that first day, I have realized that Christ freed me from a false god. What was I thinking? I would get stressed, bored, anxious, etc., bow to my idol (smoke a cigarette), and then feel okay as if I accomplished something. No, Christ's work on the cross is the only true life-sustaining accomplishment! I hope this helps you! I will pray for His accomplishment through you.

A Ten-Step Process

1: Praise God

You like smoking. It's your habit, but you know it's an addiction because you won't walk away from it. Smoking controls you. You also love Jesus, but you're unsure how to connect the gospel to your smoking habit. Where do you begin? How do you kick the habit? You first want to praise God for moving your heart to kick the habit. Whenever a person wants to change, it is a reason to praise God for the desire because it's evidence of His favor in their lives. The addicted Christian does not have to despair—only people without the gospel despair. Christians have the answer to the problems of life. As you praise God, you also want to address the idolatry in your heart practically. Idolatry is a vandalism of the heart that marginalizes the gospel. You don't want to vandalize your heart. Therefore, your goal is to elevate the gospel to the most prominent place in your life.

2: Preach the Gospel

Rose talked about connecting the gospel to her smoking addiction. What did she mean? How do you do that? "Preaching the gospel to yourself" is not a Christianized version of self-talk. Preaching the gospel to yourself is bringing your thoughts to the obedience of Christ (2 Corinthians 10:5). Preaching the gospel to yourself is an intentional focus on Christ rather than thinking about yourself or your temptations. The gospel is Christ; thus, preaching the gospel to yourself is similar to preaching Christ to yourself. As you preach Christ to yourself, you explicitly and theologically instruct yourself about what Christ did to take all your sins and give you His alien righteousness. The gospel is not magic or formulaic. Neither is it like waving a wand over your soul. It is active and intentional obedience to God. It is the opposite of addiction, which is obedience to yourself.

3: Power of the Gospel

Do you believe there is power in the gospel (Romans 1:16)? Do you understand the power of the gospel that regenerated you can also sanctify you? Do not move too quickly here. Think about it. I am not talking about a cliche or Christian-speak. There are times when you experience acute temptation that is real and dominating. Your gospel must be more than nominalism. I'm talking about "gospel-grunt-work" that empowers you in proportion to your cooperation with the Lord through the change process. You cannot live a non-gospel-centered life and expect there to be gospel-centered power to get over the humps of acute temptation. That is presumption (Psalm 19:13). People do this when the plane goes down; they reach out to God in a crisis.

> Therefore, my beloved, as you have always obeyed,
> so now, not only as in my presence but much more
> in my absence, work out your own salvation with

fear and trembling, for it is God who works in you,
both to will and to work for his good pleasure.
(Philippians 2:12-13).

4: What Is Wrong?

But each person is tempted when he is lured and
enticed by his own desire. Then desire when it has
conceived gives birth to sin, and sin when it is fully
grown brings forth death.
(James 1:14-15)

All fallen people are in crisis every second of the day, so you want to activate the power of the gospel every second of your life. The biggest problem we have is in our hearts, not our behaviors. Whatever may be between our fingers is behavioral, but we will find the cure elsewhere. This sinful desire of our hearts is the same as any external behavioral addiction. Smoking, eating too many *Happy Meals,* ongoing excessive shopping, or TV binge-watching have one thing in common: the original cause came from the heart. Because smoking has bad optics, too many folks tend to focus on the appearance of tobacco rather than the cause of smoking. Christians are susceptible to condemning smokers, which is ironic since we all have a similar kind of active worldliness in our hearts. The only difference is that our heart idols manifest in socially acceptable ways.

An example of this is the overweight person. The smoker is sabotaging his lungs, while the overeater is sabotaging his heart. There should not be a debate between smokey lungs and clogged arteries. If the choices are between smoking or eating too much, I think I would rather light up than be overweight, though neither option is wise. What is wrong with the smoker is his motive for smoking. His habit gives him something he wants. If he wants to change, he must discern and disarm this desire. Not addressing the heart motive is why modifying the behavior has a low success rate. Rose said it this way:

> Since that first day, I have realized that Christ freed me from a false god. What was I thinking? I would get stressed, bored, anxious, etc., bow to my idol (smoke a cigarette), and then feel okay as if I accomplished something. No, Christ's work on the cross is the only true life-sustaining accomplishment!

First, she had to address her wrong motives. If she did not eliminate those causes, she would light up when stress, boredom, or anxiousness returned. Let's say she quit smoking but did not repent of her heart's ruling motives. The smoking behavior does stop, but she is still an idolator. Because she is an idolator, she will find another way to comfort her troubled soul when difficulty comes, probably swapping one idol for the next. Perhaps she gains weight in response to stopping smoking. She did not change at the fundamental core of her being. The idolater continues to worship something other than God. So, what happened here? She switched idols: smoking to overeating.

5: Repent Rightly

If you believe smoking is a sin, you need to repent of it, which means getting to the real issue if you want to change. You need to dig deeper. You have to identify, isolate, and repent of the right things, the things that led to smoking cigarettes. If you get the heart idolatry piece right, there will be proper motivation, hope, faith, encouragement, excitement, and eventual freedom. Here are a few examples of possible heart motivations of the addicted person. Perhaps some of these things are triggers for you. Maybe you can add other things to your list. You'll notice these are not exclusive to the addicted smoker.

Self-reliance	Fear	Unbelief
Comfort	Anger	Criticalness
Envy	Unforgiveness	Laziness
Unhappiness	Jealousy	Bitterness
Self-righteousness	Ignorance	Discontent

All of these conditions in the heart represent reasons for smoking (or whatever your addiction may be). All addicted people find some of these things hanging out in their hearts. Smoking masks these underlying idols. I appeal to you to critically assess yourself to see what idols are lurking in your heart. It would help to have an open dialogue with someone who knows you. Overcoming an addiction alone is nearly impossible.

6: Motivate with Kindness

Condemnation is the worst thing you can do for an addicted person. Self-righteous attitudes toward fallen soldiers are ludicrous. Everybody is addicted to something. Being shocked when someone fails is a misunderstanding of the human condition. If you want to help him, encourage him. Paul said the kindness of God leads to change. God's kind favor to you resulted in your repentance. If you want to help an addicted person change, show God's kindness to him. Model the gospel by encouraging him. You can also show kindness by praying with him—not just for him, but with him. Another way to demonstrate compassion is by your patience (1 Thessalonians 5:14). The addicted person will likely fail, and you will be disappointed. Paul said to keep an eye on yourself as you help the caught person (Galatians 6:2). Give him a shoulder to cry on and an ear that listens.

- Do not condemn.
- Do not be surprised.
- Encourage your friend.
- Show God's kindness.
- Pray for and with him.
- Be patient with him.
- Be slow to speak and quick to listen.

The Lord models the gospel to you in these ways: He is kind, encourages, and intercedes. He also sympathizes and listens when you speak. One of the best gifts you can give the addicted is your imitation of Christ. "Therefore be imitators of God, as beloved children" (Ephesians 5:1).

7: It Takes a Community

Sin festers and grows in a dark and silent world. To overcome the ever-present pull to be drawn into it, you must walk in the light while talking about the light. One way to do this is by letting others know what God is doing in your life. It takes a community. There are three good reasons to let others know about your struggle and your need for their help:

1. It will extend the net of care and accountability. The more who know what you are doing, the more people there are to serve you by talking directly to you.
2. The more you talk about what God is doing for you, the more motivated you will be to keep moving in the right direction, assuring your ability to learn, remember, and apply what God is teaching you.
3. The more you share what God is doing, the more others around you will be encouraged to change and grow. God's grace becomes contagious as it spills into other people's lives.

You must tell your friends what is happening and what you are doing about it. These friends must not be people-pleasers. They must be grace-empowered, God-honoring, neighbor-loving, truth-tellers. Real friends should be compassionately critical during this season of your life.

> Faithful are the wounds of a friend; profuse are the kisses of an enemy.
>
> (Proverbs 27:6)

8: Change of Plans

Talk to your friends about all the ways some people and situations have been sources of temptation to smoke. Get specific. Examine your life.

1. What are those trigger points?
2. Tell others about them, and ask them to bring them up when you meet.
3. When are you most tempted to smoke?
4. Who are the people in your life who make it easy for you to smoke? Some of these tempters could be your friends. Others may be secondary associations who are difficult, painful, or frustrating people. When you're around them, you are tempted to smoke. Enjoyable and disappointing friends serve a similar purpose: they tempt you to smoke.
5. Locations may also tempt you to smoke. Think about places and events that have been sources of temptation. Consider rearranging calendars, friends, venues, travel routes, and anything else that may be a source of temptation.

Repentance means to "go the other way." This concept of turning around could be broad in its sweep and cause hurt feelings. Change is often painful, but the growth that will accompany repentance is worth the pain of change.

9: Love God and Neighbor

Sin is doggedly self-focused. It will turn on you to devour you (1 Peter 5:8). Love, on the other hand, is always other-focused. Sin leaves you wanting, but love satisfies. Sin eats at you until nothing is left but a shell, while love fills you to the brim (Psalm 23:5). You want to replace your bad habit of self-centeredness with the proper biblical habit of other-centeredness. Stop making it all about you. Paul talked about putting off and putting on (Ephesians 4:22-24). It's time to put off your self-centered lifestyle and put on a God-centered one. Practically serving others is an excellent, gospel-centered idea. It is the opposite of what an addicted person does. It is impossible to quit smoking and not fill your heart or time with other things. God created you to worship from the heart while manifesting that worship to His world. Something will always rule your heart and your behaviors. The Creator created you to worship Him and love others (Matthew 22:36-40). The gospel is the perfect picture of what that looks like in a fallen world. How can you spread the fame of God by actively serving others in your community? Ask God to give you ideas.

10: Pray Without Ceasing

Rose said she fell on her knees and cried like a baby. Her example is the best way to describe what your life must resemble. It's a praying life. I cannot overstate this. You will have to live on your knees. As you pray, enlist others to pray for you. Bombard the throne of God with relentless petitions for merciful grace. There is grace for the humble, and He loves lavishing His children with much of it (James 4:6). Here is the good news: If you are considering quitting smoking, you have correctly positioned yourself for God's other-worldly favor to come to you.

Call to Action

1. What will you do next?
2. What is your detailed, specific plan for change?
3. Who will you invite into this journey?

6

Their Sin, Your Health

The interplay between our physical and spiritual selves needs responsible engagement within the Christian community, especially how a conflict between two people can lead to diminishing health. I have counseled many spouses with declining health that often paralleled the sinful relationships with their spouses. In nearly every case, their spouses had corrupting speech patterns: demanding, angry, manipulative, controlling, and other forms of selfish anger, including relational passivity and neglect (Ephesians 4:29).

The Interplay

Blessed is the man against whom the LORD counts no iniquity, and in whose spirit there is no deceit. For when I kept silent, my bones wasted away through my groaning all day long. For day and night your hand was heavy upon me; my strength was dried up as by the heat of summer.

(Psalm 32:2-4)

Though the relationship between our spiritual and physical selves is subjective when applied to a particular couple, there is a biblical precedent regarding the adverse occurrence of sin and its biological effects. David was living in sin. He would not confess his sins, and his lack of honest confession took a toll on his body. Physical atrophy is one of the effects of sin. In David's situation, repentance led to biological restoration. However, this problem becomes exponentially more complicated when another person's unconfessed, unforgiven, and unrepented sins continue within a relationship. Like David, I can repent and find restoration if my sin affects my health. If someone else's sin affects my health, I am at the mercy of that other person to remove their sin from our relationship. In some marriages, the wicked spouse does not repent, leaving the offended spouse vulnerable.

Adverse Effects

I was listening to a podcast from The People's Pharmacy that reminded me of this concept. A podcast where Joe and Terry Graedon share their perspectives on health-related issues. Here is an excerpt from the podcast, which is not what that episode was about but part of their usual eclectic introduction, where they talked about current headlines and medical updates.

Social isolation is a recognized risk factor for morbidity and mortality, but interacting negatively with family, friends, and neighbors has drawbacks. A ten-year study of nearly 10,000 middle-aged Danes found that those who had acrimonious relationships were far more likely to die from cancer, heart disease, liver disease, or accidents. The research estimates that frequent arguments or stressful demands from close contacts, such as partners or children, could increase the risk of death from any cause by at least 50 percent. Constant arguing had *an unusually adverse effect, and men who were out of work seemed to be most vulnerable to this stress. Investigators speculate that conflict management skills could help people lead longer, healthier, and happier lives.*

Considering Connections

I do not believe a valid argument would dismiss the connection and interplay between our physical and spiritual selves. The real issue to consider is to what degree a person is affected by the ongoing, unrepented sin of another person. This issue is both genuine and subjective. I have experienced this when public speaking. In the early years of ministry, I had difficulty dealing with fear when it was time to speak. This fear had a measurable, physical effect on my body. A spiritual issue—fear of man—played out in my physicality. My body settled down when the speaking event ended, and everything was normal. There are other physical/spiritual interplays in my life, and I am sure you have your stories too. For example, exercise is not a cure-all for depression, but it can be part of the overall solution for some people who are depressed. In other situations, I have recommended physical exercise in the context of a person's spiritual well-being. I have seen measurable results with a few individuals who have added this discipline into their daily routines.

A Path Forward

This discussion stirs a few concerns, especially from a person who is in a non-redemptive relationship. Here are four of those possible concerns:

- Am I a victim?
- What about the grace of God in unrepentant relationships?

- If my spouse is affecting my health, may I leave?
- Where do I find help?

The Victim Problem

So we do not lose heart. Though our outer nature is wasting away, our inner nature is being renewed day by day.

(2 Corinthians 4:16)

In the grander scope of the human condition, we all are victims. The sin of Adam and Eve created a death march toward the grave (Romans 5:12). We are victims of the cosmic crime between God and man, and God justly punishes us for such offenses. There is a physical depreciation at conception because death is part of the equation. Like driving a new car off the car lot, it becomes of lesser value after you take it home. Sin is constantly affecting us in atrophic ways. We are in a constant degenerating condition because of human depravity; Paul called it wasting away. You must determine if your declining health is the typical wasting away process of growing older or if a toxic relationship is making things worse. It is probably both if you're in a sinful relationship. You are growing older, your body is breaking down, and an acrimonious relationship speeds up that decaying process. You should consider both possibilities and do what you must to stay healthy.

Grace for This

Because we are victims of Adamic sin, the impact of corruption on our lives can be degenerative. Thus, we must talk about the transformative power of the gospel that God gave us. It is important not to lose heart, as Paul said. God is merciful. He does not leave us to fend for ourselves. He always provides a way of escape when offenses, whether Adamic, ours, or from others, bring temptation into our lives (1 Corinthians 10:13). The possibility of escape is the good news because a person could be tempted to give up, choosing not to access these means of grace the Lord gives us. The temptation to quit and not to fight is always real and enticing. Many adults give up the fight against sin and let their bodies go. They feel the gravitational pull of death on them, and rather than finishing strong, they yield to the ever-increasing physical and spiritual tugs. Whether it is the degenerative effect of the sins of Adam or the sins within your interpersonal relationships that you are uniquely bound to, there is grace for these matters.

Get Away

If I were in a situation where my spouse's unrelenting meanness and other sins were affecting my health, one of the things I would consider is separation. Of course, this response should motivate me to wade through these waters with carefulness. Biblical grounds for separation, which leads to divorce, are adultery and desertion. A sinful, unrepentant spouse does not fall within those parameters, but this does not leave you helpless. For example, if a person is physically or sexually sinning against you, we are talking about crimes and sins, which are punishable by law. If someone physically or sexually sins against you, do not hesitate to report the crime to the authorities while escaping the situation. If someone knows about these sin crimes, they must report them immediately. If someone is sinning in these ways, there is one option: you run and report the sinning criminal to the authorities. This responsibility is not negotiable. For Christians, there is a process for sins that adversely impact a person's spiritual and physical well-being, and that method may include separation.

Help Is Here

If your brother sins against you, go and tell him his fault, between you and him alone. If he listens to you, you have gained your brother. But if he does not listen, take one or two others along with you, that every charge may be established by the evidence of two or three witnesses.

(Matthew 18:15-16)

The first call to action is to appeal to the abuser—if it is possible. In some situations, this is not possible or wise. For example, I am not talking about sexual or physical sin. In those cases, you do not appeal first; you run from the violence. In other situations, where your physicality is not in the kind of threat that sexual and physical sin cause, you appeal to the person to stop. If the person does not stop, you call for help. Do not try to persuade a sinful, prideful, domineering person to cease to be domineering on your own. The Lord gave us a process for these mean people. You have an advocate in the body of Christ—an excellent means of grace—to come alongside the victims of sin. Many people will read this and say, "Yes, but my church does not have the means, competency, or concern to help me." In some situations, we have failed the body of Christ. I am critiquing myself here, too. I am speaking about us—the body of the Lord Jesus Christ as manifested in our local churches. Many Christians live in marriages where the church does not pursue, help, or hold sinners accountable.

A Limited Church

This reality is where we must be careful. It would be misguided to lay people's sinfulness in the church's lap. That is not a reasonable charge, nor is it biblical. Many churches are stellar in the fight against sin. They are like me in that the need for help is far greater than any person's or institution's ability to provide. It would be placing the cause of the problem on our local churches. Undoubtedly, the church can and should do a better job, but the real issue is how sinful people do not want to change. It is similar to the hospital: the help is available, but the person who needs the help must access it. Many, if not most, of the people who live in unrepentant sin are defiant and elusive. They are not part of a local church, which puts the local church at a disadvantage.

> So whoever knows the right thing to do and fails to do it, for him it is sin.
>
> (James 4:17)

Power to Change

I have never met someone who truly wanted to change and could not change. If a wicked person wants to stop his wickedness, the transformative gospel, with or without the local church, has enough power for him to do that. If you are in a sinful relationship, do not keep silent. Find a way to speak out; go for help. Our ministry has been a refuge and a lifeline to many people who have found nowhere to turn. We are not the local church or a replacement for the local church, but we can complement the local church by bringing care to the body of Christ. We also have been a means of grace to help churches learn how to be helpful in their discipleship practices. I permit you to share our content and ministry with your church. It also may be possible for you to find a counselor who can come alongside you to help walk you through a dangerous relationship. Do not try to fight the fight against sin alone, whether it is your sin or the sin of others. In the context of this chapter, I'm speaking of the sins of others. Your spiritual and physical life will be affected in proportion to the amount, degree, and type of sin waging war against you.

Call to Action

1. Are you in a strained relationship? What practical things can you do to change the situation?
2. Are you safe in your relationship? If not, you must leave—at least for a season, while letting others know what is happening.
3. If your health is declining, what are some things that you can do to help yourself get better?

7

Overcoming Insomnia

I have struggled with insomnia—intermittently—since 2003. It has been so long that I rarely talk about it unless someone asks. I resigned myself to insomnia as a way of life. My insomnia is like an unwanted friend who periodically shows up late at night. He makes his visits without warning. I can go for weeks with relatively good sleep, though I have probably not had a sound sleep the way a child enjoys sleep since I was a child.

When All Else Fails

Our children—when they were young—could sleep anywhere. They awoke fully refreshed and ready to go about their day. They never complained about a poor night's rest. I do not believe it occurred to them that a person cannot sleep well. When my poor sleeping season comes, I can go for weeks without sleeping all night. It might be 3 AM before I finally give up the fight. Most nights, I toss and turn until 5 AM or later. I became angry during the first few years as I tossed and turned. I finally grew weary of going through the anger ritual, so I repented.

I then asked God to give me the strength for the day after a rough night of sleeplessness. The Lord is faithful; He provides what I need to get through a day, even when I've had two or three hours of sleep. Though my sleeping cycles have improved dramatically, now and again, the nights are long. I am mostly okay when the sleep debt is high because it motivates me to become an active practitioner in grace appropriation, a fancy way of saying, "Dear God, help me." If you struggle with a lack of sleep, my best tip is for you to pray, asking the Lord to give you what you need to endure seasons of deprivation.

Insomnia is like depression in the sense that each person is different, and there is no way to provide a universal solution for all its causes. My best response is, "I do not know why you do not sleep well." I have some ideas, but I am not dogmatic about them—any more than I am dogmatic about the causes of depression. Life can be mysterious for Adamic people, requiring a level of comfortableness with the un-resolvableness of challenging problems. But we do need practical help, and I want to make a few suggestions. With the backdrop of prayer as your constant go-to and your willingness to live in life's mysteries, let's begin by considering these two things:

- What kind of person are you?
- What do you need to add or eliminate from your life?

The Gift of Faith

Sleep is connected to faith. In a real and practical way, a lack of sleep is a trust issue. It reminds me of Jesus sleeping in a boat during a dark and stormy night (Mark 4:38). To sleep well is to trust well. You can substitute the word security or stability for the word faith. A child in a secure environment, for example, where he is not worried about anything, is not distracted from sleeping well. A child in a chaotic home, where arguing and drama are the norms, has more difficulty being at peace. Worry, anxiety, drama, chaos, and instability interrupt a person's faith, which interferes with their sleep. The object of your faith is what gives strength to your faith. The solution for weak faith is not more faith but to figure out what keeps you from focusing on the object of your faith. Faith in Jesus, the object, is broken, weakening you. This Adamic problem leads to the question: What keeps you from appropriating Christ in your life, redemptively improving your sleep? Perhaps sharing three of my faith interrupters will help.

My Faith Interrupters

SELF-RELIANCE: I struggle with self-sufficiency, which is doing things under my strength rather than trusting the Lord. 2 Corinthians 1:8-9 teaches how to rely on the Lord rather than ourselves. God sent trouble into Paul's life to break him from his nasty, self-reliant habit. The irony is that my insomnia is God's merciful intruder, sent to help me break a bad habit. I'm learning to rely on the Lord regarding the things I cannot fix. In this case, the thing I cannot seem to fix is insomnia. If you wrestle with things in your life that appear to be unfixable, like fear, anxiousness, anger, or despair, you are not relying on the Lord. If you do not break the habit of self-reliant insomnia, for example, you may always entertain this nightly bedfellow.

THE GIFTED CURSE: In the television series *Monk,* there was a repeated theme when folks experienced Monk's unique gift for solving crimes. They would say, "It is a gift," to which Monk would always follow with, "And a curse." Your greatest strength is your greatest weakness. Oswald Chambers said, "An unguarded strength is a double weakness." Connected to my problem of self-reliance is the gift of an active mind, which is a perpetual, overworked, whirring processor. I do not know how to stop my brain from thinking. My always on the move mind is most active when the Lord gives me a thought, even at night. I call them my nightly visitors who latch onto my brain. Most of the time, it is a thought about creative ideas or better ways to run our ministry. Once my mind latches onto one of these creatures of the night, it speeds up to the point that I cannot stop thinking about it until I exhaust the idea.

COMMUNAL TENSION: I do not do well when people are angry with me. It is hard for me to ignore tension in my closest relationships. I am not necessarily bothered by internet friends who say nasty things about me, but it is different with those who are friends. Though this circle is small, tension affects my thought life. People become big, and God becomes small. I can spend more time thinking about the individual who is angry with me than my Lord, who owns me. However, when I see the difficult person as God's mercy, it helps to break my tendency to self-reliance.

15 Tips to Consider

If you struggle with insomnia, I recommend you consider what might be happening in your mind when your planned sleep is slipping away. Here are a few questions that will help.

- What is happening in your life, relationships, or situations?
- What are you thinking about that keeps you awake?
- What is bothering you? Who is bothering you?
- What are some things you can remove from your thought life? How can you take your thoughts captive?

Spend time thinking and discussing these questions over the next few months. (Just not at night.) As you begin to discern your faith interrupters, drill down into these problems, with plans to take those thoughts captive and subject them to the obedience of Christ (2 Corinthians 10:3-5).

Process of Elimination

I have spent many years thinking about insomnia. I am not an expert, but I have learned a few things. I have also implemented some ideas that help me battle sleep issues. What I do is not a prescription for you. My list is different from yours. I am not a doctor, but a regular guy who does have occasional insomnia problems. The main thing I do is pray. That is your best action item for sleeplessness and gracefully enduring the next day. These first seven things are standard practices that nearly every health professional believes are musts if you want a better quality of life. These are non-negotiable, not just for a sleep problem but for all potential health concerns.

1. **EAT HEALTHILY:** I am not talking about a diet but a lifestyle. Eating well, which includes what you drink, should be a daily habit.
2. **EXERCISE OFTEN:** Find a workout plan that fits your lifestyle. You must be active.
3. **PROPER WEIGHT:** Most people don't want to hear this, but you have to take action if you weigh too much.
4. **NO SMOKING, MODERATE ALCOHOL:** I have a disdain for tobacco and have never enjoyed alcohol, so these two items are not a problem for me.
5. **PROPER SLEEP:** I am working on this one. I take power naps during the day, anywhere from twenty minutes to two hours—depending on what is needed. If I go too long without enough sleep, I sin more. Proper sleep reduces sin problems.
6. **CLEAR CONSCIENCE:** Your inner voice can keep you awake at night, which makes it imperative that you do not have hidden sin. If you are wrestling with sin, you must let someone know. Do not be intellectually dishonest by talking about

remedies for insomnia while holding on to sinful habituations.

7. **WORK HARD:** When you work, work hard. Do not slouch around all day and go to bed. Exhaustion is one of the benefits of exercise, in that it wears you out to where you are ready for bed. Work your body hard so that when it is time to sleep, you will have your best shot at sleeping.

8. **REMOVE THE BLUE LIGHT:** Technology is one of the biggest culprits to poor sleep habits. Devices have a blue light that tricks your brain into thinking it is daytime. During the evening, your melatonin rises, which helps you sleep. The device's blue light tells your brain it is not nighttime, which reduces your melatonin. Lowering a child's melatonin at bedtime is a huge problem. Sadly, rather than moderating device use, parents put them on medication. Use the computer's software that changes the screen at dusk by filtering the blue light. Changing my screen at night is a big help since most of my job is on the computer.

9. **WHITE NOISE:** I have two forms of white noise that blow air: room-temperature air from a fan and hot air from podcasts. For several years, I have gone to bed wearing earbuds. I listen to interviews, books, and sports, which are not worth remembering. I'm not a super sports fan, so listening to trivial sports information distracts me from the important things that tend to keep me awake.

10. **BLACKOUT MATERIAL:** Our bedroom curtains have blackout material on the back. The Lord cursed the Egyptians with a darkness that could be felt (Exodus 10:21), and we have nearly reproduced that darkness in our bedroom.

11. **KEEP QUIET:** Lucia has to go to bed before I do. If she is up and moving around, it is nearly impossible for

me to sleep. For the record, she loves this tip.

12. **STOP EATING:** If I stop eating and drinking by 6 PM, I have my best chance of sleeping. As I have aged, the need to go to the bathroom at night has increased.

13. **MIDNIGHT SNACKS:** Typically, when I cannot sleep, I want to eat. Late-night eating not only adds poundage but also keeps me awake. Eating late as an answer to insomnia is not a good idea.

14. **HEALTH CHECK:** I have blood work done twice yearly. From these visits, I can adapt my health plan every six months.

15. **BE ON TIME:** A standard, though not rigid, sleep schedule is a good idea. I try to be in bed by 10 PM, hoping to get eight hours of sleep.

The Gift of Sleep

Sleep, like faith, is a gift from the Lord. He controls all things. He can give you the peace you need to sleep well and remove that peace, too. His sovereignty does not relieve you of your responsibility for sleep or faith, which is why your cooperation with the Lord is essential to sleep well (Philippians 2:12-13). Your cooperation ensures you have eliminated all the things hindering your sleep. If you still cannot sleep, ask the Lord to explain to you why you cannot. Use your seasons of sleeplessness to learn more about yourself while enriching your relationship with God. You may find being up late is a gift.

Call to Action

1. In what ways will you use this information to improve?
2. How can you help a friend who struggles with their sleep? You may be surprised at how many folks do not sleep well.
3. Will you invite someone into your plans for change?
4. If all else fails, listen to my podcasts.

8

The Grace of Fasting

When you consider spiritual disciplines, where does fasting rank? Most Christians pray, read, and study their Bibles regularly. Praise God! Many engage in fellowship, discipleship, and evangelism. Yet, fasting often falls lower on the list of our practiced disciplines. Why is this? I propose fasting is among the most powerful spiritual disciplines a believer can adopt, impacting their lives in ways that prayer, Bible study, and fellowship alone cannot achieve. I also propose that the significance of fasting as a means of grace in the Christian life will challenge common misconceptions and encourage us to consider its place in our pursuit of holiness.

Why Is It Vital?

The Bible consistently presents fasting as a spiritual discipline. Scripture portrays individuals fasting in times of grief, repentance, decision-making, and worship. From Moses' 40-day fast on Mount Sinai to Jesus' 40-day fast in the wilderness, the Bible places fasting at the center of our significant spiritual movements and revelations. It is a form of self-denial that helps us draw nearer to God, reminding us that our dependence should be on Him rather than on the things of this world. Through fasting, we choose to humble ourselves before God, creating a space to deny the flesh's cravings and to strengthen our spirit.

It is a discipline that encourages self-control, and unlike other spiritual disciplines, fasting intensifies our focus on God by stripping away earthly distractions. Yet, despite its importance, fasting often needs to be more frequently addressed among Christians. For most, skipping meals may seem unnecessary or unhealthy, a sentiment primarily tied to how modern culture has conditioned us to eat at regular intervals, often without considering hunger's true meaning. This unfamiliarity with genuine hunger can make fasting intimidating and daunting, which brings us to one of the key barriers to fasting: understanding what true hunger is.

Are You Hungry?

Most people have never experienced true hunger pangs, those legitimate signals of physical need for nourishment. When people speak of hunger, they typically describe a habitual response—what their bodies feel when they deviate from their normal eating ritual. They develop a hunger habituation through routine, which is nothing more than muscle memory gaslighting them into believing they must eat now or perish. This routine feeling of hunger is the body signaling its preference, not a real biological need for sustenance. Most people in first-world countries have never had any experiences with legitimate hunger pangs.

They are hesitant to fast because they fear the discomfort of skipping a meal or going without food for an entire day. True hunger only sets in after many days or weeks without food. Missing a meal or a day of eating doesn't produce legitimate hunger pangs. Understanding this distinction is foundational, as it reframes fasting as an attainable practice rather than an arduous deprivation. The body adjusts to fasting quickly, and once it breaks free from a meal-based schedule, physical hunger largely subsides. This adjustment allows us to focus on the spiritual side of fasting without constant reminders of physical discomfort.

Pathway to Self-control

One of the most profound spiritual benefits of fasting is the self-control it cultivates. When we fast, we deny our natural desires and teach our bodies submission to a higher purpose. This exercise in self-control directly opposes the culture around us, which encourages indulging in comfort wherever you can find it and the accompanying instant gratification. My journey with fasting began during my Bible college years. A friend and I decided to fast for 24 hours, hoping for a spiritual breakthrough. That first experience was, by most measures, unsuccessful. I spent the entire day thinking about food, making the fast feel more like a test of endurance than a spiritual practice. But over time, as I practiced fasting, I learned how to overcome this initial fixation on food and transition to a place of spiritual focus and growth.

Years later, when dating my wife, Lucia, we committed to fasting together to build self-control and strengthen our relationship. We would fast one week every month, relying on water alone. This rhythm of fasting proved invaluable in teaching us both self-control—an essential quality in a dating relationship and one that has continued to benefit our marriage. By regularly setting aside food, we learn to control our desires, whether it's eating or other areas of life. Self-control is like a muscle that grows through discipline and practice. When we master our physical appetite, we become better equipped to exercise self-control in areas like speech and time management.

Spiritual and Physical

Fasting offers not only spiritual growth but also mental and physical benefits. Many experience increased clarity, sharper focus, and improved energy during extended fasts. Without the constant demands of digestion, our bodies can redirect energy toward other functions, including mental and spiritual pursuits. After the initial three days of fasting, the body enters a state where the need for food fades into the background, and hunger is no longer the primary focus. You do not hunger after three days. In this state, the mind becomes more alert, and tasks seem more manageable.

I have experienced some of my most productive seasons during fasting regarding mental clarity and spiritual insight. The simplicity of fasting is freeing, allowing us to channel our energy toward prayer, study, or reflection without the distractions of food preparation, eating, or even grocery shopping. For some, intermittent fasting has become a popular practice. While intermittent fasting (such as restricting eating to a four or 12-hour window) can be beneficial for weight management and digestion, it does not provide the same spiritual benefits as traditional fasting. Intermittent fasting focuses more on physical health, but a biblical fast involves denying food for spiritual growth.

Types of Fasting

Fasting can take different forms depending on one's circumstances, goals, and experience level. Here are some common approaches:

- **WATER-ONLY FAST:** This is the most challenging but also the most effective. It involves drinking only water and is typically done for an extended period.
- **WATER AND JUICE FAST:** For those who find it difficult to go without food, adding juice can provide necessary nutrients without compromising the

essence of fasting. Bone broth is an excellent choice.

- **PARTIAL FASTING:** This practice involves abstaining from specific meals or foods. Daniel's fast in the Bible, during which he consumed only vegetables and water, is an example of a partial fast.
- **SHORTER FASTS:** One to three-day fasts are often harder because the body is still adjusting and craving food. Longer fasts (10 days or more) can be easier in many respects as the body adapts and the desire for food diminishes. Your body will take the hint and not bother you any longer, freeing you from the desire to eat.

Practical Tips for Fasting

For those new to fasting, it's helpful to remember a few tips to make the experience more fruitful and sustainable.

- **START SLOWLY:** To learn what fasting entails, begin with a 24-hour fast. As you grow confident, you may increase the duration. However, remember that your body "will not leave you alone" because you have trained it to eat, and it will remind you of your habit.
- **CREATE A FASTING-FRIENDLY SCHEDULE:** Plan your first few fasts when you can rest, such as a weekend. This strategy allows you to deal with physical adjustments without added responsibilities.
- **STAY HYDRATED:** Drinking water during a fast is vital. It helps curb hunger pangs and keeps you energized.
- **EXPECT RESISTANCE FROM YOUR BODY:** Initially, your body may "complain" as it adjusts. With practice, however, the body becomes more accustomed to fasting. Your body will fight to stay alive. Don't worry; you will be okay if it stops "requesting" food.
- **EMBRACE THE SPIRITUAL DISCIPLINE:** Fasting isn't just about physical endurance. Use the time to pray,

meditate on Scripture, or engage in other spiritual disciplines that draw you closer to God.

- **Toxin Elimination:** As your fast moves into three to five days, you may experience body odor because you have given your body a chance to do something other than digest food. It has time to heal by eliminating those things that are not good for you. Your tongue will also become chalky. Though your breath will smell, it will be exhilarating to know your body is doing what the Lord designed it to do: care for itself.

Understanding the Barriers

One of the greatest challenges in fasting is overcoming the mental and spiritual barriers. During the first three days, you will likely experience a battle with physical cravings. But beyond this point, fasting becomes a mental challenge. As your bodily desire for food subsides, you start focusing on your mental and spiritual needs. Fasting forces us to address the "false hunger" in our lives—the cravings that arise from internal heart cravings. As we abstain from food, we uncover the things we often turn to for comfort rather than relying on God. Fasting reveals the idols we may have unwittingly nurtured. The spiritual growth we gain from fasting reaches far beyond self-denial. By fasting, we position ourselves to hear God's voice more clearly, seek His will, and tangibly depend on His strength. When our need for physical nourishment is set aside, our desire for spiritual nourishment intensifies.

The Grace Benefits

Fasting fosters a deeper relationship with God and transforms us on multiple levels.

- **Increased Self-Control:** As mentioned, fasting develops our ability to exercise restraint over our desires. This practiced restraint through fasting will spill into other areas where we need self-control.

- **ENHANCED SPIRITUAL FOCUS:** The hunger for food is replaced by a hunger for God, enhancing our prayer life and devotion.
- **CLARITY AND DISCERNMENT:** Many report heightened clarity in their decision-making and greater sensitivity to God's leading.
- **FREEDOM FROM DISTRACTIONS:** Fasting eliminates the distractions that often pull us away from time with God, offering undistracted time for spiritual growth.
- **PRACTICAL BENEFITS:** A few pluses include more time, increased energy, and financial savings. Imagine not having to shop, prepare a meal, eat, clean the dishes, or eliminate what you had for dinner.

This newfound time can be redirected toward activities that build faith, such as prayer, Bible study, or serving others. You can redirect the freedom gained from fasting toward spiritual investments that bring eternal rewards. Our lives are deeply tied to food in ways we may not realize, and setting food aside can provide spiritual and practical benefits.

The Warnings

It's essential to remember that fasting is not for everyone and requires careful consideration. Some people may have medical conditions that make fasting inadvisable. Always consult a medical provider before beginning any type of fast, especially if you have health concerns. Moreover, fasting should never become a performance or a source of pride. Jesus warned against fasting for the sake of outward appearance. Instead, fasting should be a private matter between you and God, done with humility and reverence.

Call to Action

1. What are your thoughts about fasting? Will you share them with a friend?
2. Have you ever fasted? Will you speak with a friend about how it went? Perhaps they have fasted, too, making your conversation an inspiring time of reflecting on God's grace.
3. If you have not fasted, perhaps after consulting with your trusted friends and healthcare providers, you can strategize how to make fasting a part of your spiritual journey.

9

A Praying Life

Prayer is every believer's desire and opportunity, but many Christians struggle to have a consistent and dynamic prayer life. That's why I want to share eight practical tips to help and guide you as you think about one of the most crucial things we can do regarding our relationship with God. These thoughts are what I told a friend many years ago when he asked about praying well. Here is his original question.

On Praying Well

I have a question regarding the daily discipline of prayer, hoping to gain a perspective from others. Since God saved me about ten years ago, I have been deeply convinced to pray. As a new convert, I asked others how they prayed and read books on this vital subject. Unfortunately, a legalistic environment had poorly nurtured my ideas about prayer for too many years. It became an issue. If I missed my morning prayer time, I would be depressed all day because I believed I had lost God's favor. I would not have said that, but it is how I lived. I still struggle with it today. Over the last few years, as I have begun to rethink and understand the gospel better, I have tried to remind myself, by God's grace, that grace through faith leads to salvation.

Even when I have not prayed as I ought, I have said, "Lord, thank you that I am no less your son. Though I'm rushing right now, I can have joy in believing, regardless of my prayer life." Though those things are real, my deep conviction to pray has never left, and I often find it hard (though I hate to say it) to fit prayer into my life. At this season, I feel swamped. My schedule makes it hard to pray consistently. If I let the day get away from me, it is hard to stop and spend quality time in prayer. This routine can drag on, and I begin to feel worse and worse.

- Do you think I should toughen up, live on less sleep, and get up early?
- Should I rearrange my work schedule if I can?
- Should I learn to turn every distraction off at some point during the day other than in the morning and seek God then?

I understand that Jesus saved me and is always with me. My relationship with the Lord is the greatest treasure of my life, and I am willing to change what I have to. I would love some help with my prayer life.
                                        – Struggling Friend

Our Common Struggle

An inconsistent or non-existent prayer life reminds me of athletes who do not stretch before they run. Most runners do not. Running is the main thing; stretching is a mundane precursor to the main thing. When it comes to praying well, engaging your day is the main thing; prayer is the mundane warm-up, but if it is valued, it will make the race a more enjoyable experience. Though we know this, we may be similar to my friend, struggling to appreciate prayer enough to implement it into the fabric of our daily lives. I have given much thought to my prayer struggle because I have experienced it since the Lord regenerated me in 1984. I want to share with you what I told my friend, the eight things that come to mind when I consider improving my prayer life. I hope they will help you in your walk with the Lord.

Stop Praying: Start Talking

First, I recommend you move the word prayer to the back of your vocabulary list—at least for now—and replace it with talk or talking to the Lord. The Lord is a person, not an object. I think sometimes we think about the Lord the same way other religions bow to their objects and idols. Bowing and talking to an object is like talking to a signpost. It is an impersonal, unidirectional communication that is not warm or reciprocated. Prayer can connote that attitude for some individuals: God is a distant deity rather than a sympathizing friend. This pagan worldview makes prayer colder than ice and chore-like rather than a lively, robust conversation between two people.

Be God's Friend

Abraham believed God, which was counted to him as righteousness—and he was called a friend of God.
(James 2:23)

I recommend you use the word "friend" for how you think about the Lord. You can think about Him in many ways, which you should, but what if you make the word friend common speak when you think about Him? Jesus wants us to think of Him as a friend (John 15:15). This friendship helps to soften the righteous rigidity from a former legalistic presupposition and worldview. The Lord is both transcendent and immanent. You hold Him in awe, power, majesty, and wonder, and He understands your most painful struggles and frustrating temptations. God is not like us, and He is near us. Based on what my friend said about his legalism, I imagine it's more comfortable for him to think of the Lord in a courtroom rather than a living room. He will have to reverse this, especially when thinking about prayer.

Unlimited Talk Time

Though you may not be married, I will use a marriage analogy here. In the context of this chapter, I think about the Lord in a similar way that I think about my wife. She is my friend, my best friend in life. I talk to her throughout the day, at different times, and through various means: phone, text, and verbally. I think about her often because she is my partner. I have pictures of her on my desk and in my heart. This ever-present awareness is how I engage the Lord. I do not phone or text Him, but I regularly engage Him throughout my day with short messages (prayers) or more protracted talks (prayers). You must make this your habit.

Talk about Everything

If you have an unlimited talk plan with the Lord (which you do), don't worry about using up your minutes: Talk to Him about everything at any time. Isn't this what you do with best friends? If you have an idea, share it with the Lord. You will never talk too much to God. Create that kind of talk habit. Let Him become your best friend with whom you want to share all your thoughts. That means you are asking Him for things to come and thanking Him for things provided. Tomorrow, as you go to work, ponder your life; thank Him for what He brings to mind. Talk to Him. Ask questions. Practice gratitude.

Structure and Spontaneity

Sometimes, my wife and I cannot find adequate time to talk. Even so, that does not alter our relationship. Recently, we chatted from 11:30 PM to 1:30 AM. We talked about life, family, friends, and how to live well with others. It was a great conversation. It was satisfying and spontaneous. We also have scheduled date times analogous to dedicated prayer times in a "closet." Typically, we will go to a diner or coffee shop. It is rarely about the place but about being with each other. We are friends who talk to each other at different times, in different ways, about different things. The Lord is your friend, and you must speak to Him in various ways about various things. Some of your time with Him will be structured, dedicated prayer times, but most of your talk times should be spontaneous. If you pray in a structured context for fifteen or twenty minutes, you will have fourteen to eighteen hours of random talk time left to enjoy.

Free from Legalism

Legalism is the bane of praying. It will choke the life out of your prayers while filling you with doubt, striving, and frustration. Praying every day at the same time in the same place is not a bad idea, but it should not be a hill of legalism to die on because it is impossible. As much as I love my wife, I cannot maintain that kind of commitment to her. Prayer is not a competition with yourself to be perfect but only part of your relationship with the Lord. If your time with Him morphs to the point of legalistic conditionalism, your relationship will struggle. If you are able to pray every morning at a particular time, by all means, pray then. But do not let that time define your relationship with the Lord. Do not think He is displeased with you if you miss it. That is not how you define a loving relationship.

Be Dependent

One of the ways I talk to God is when I write. I write as though the Lord is at my elbow. I ask Him about the content I am creating. For example, I asked Him what I should say about praying. When I finished, I thanked Him for how He shaped my thoughts. That is one way I can demonstrate my dependence on Him. Think about how you can create opportunities to show your dependence on Him. Ask Him for help regarding all matters of life, big and small. Some of those times will be structured prayer moments, but most will happen in the milieu: the day-to-day contexts in which you live. "In the milieu" praying means keeping in step with the Spirit. With each step you take, your best Friend is at your side.

Enjoy a Variety

There are at least four kinds of prayers you might want to consider: Wow, Help, Thanks, and Please. Think through how you can implement all of them into your life.

- *"Wow, dear Lord, you are amazing."* Wow-type praying is when you are overwhelmed by the Lord's kindness, greatness, and all-powerfulness. When the finite tries to wrap his brain around the Infinite, he can only prostrate himself on the ground in stunned amazement.

- *"Help me, dear Lord. I need you."* This type of praying gets at the heart of your desires and needs. You are in that place again where you need help and know the only person who can help is God Almighty, so you ask Him to impose Himself into your life and situations.

- *"Thanks, Lord. You are so kind to me."* Then, there are gratitude prayers. This one should be rolling off your tongue every waking hour. There is never enough time on any given day to thank the Lord for all you have experienced from Him. Gratitude praying should be the most frequent praying you do.

- *"Please help my friend."* One of the highest honors you can bestow on a friend is to take their needs to the King of the universe. This kind of praying is Christlike, as you imitate the One who intercedes for us. Whether in times of structured or spontaneous moments, earnest prayer for others is a gracious gift to your friends and a sweet aroma before the Lord.

Call to Action

1. Stop right now and talk to the Lord. Say something to Him. Right now!
2. Do you experience the Lord more in the courtroom or the living room? Why did you answer the way you did?
3. Ask the Lord to change your talk plan to an unlimited plan.
4. After you finish this chapter, thank the Lord for what you read and share a useful thought with Him.
5. Where is your structured place of prayer? If you do not have one, create one.
6. If you pray and have a good day, did you have a good day because you prayed? What if you did not pray and had a bad day? Did you have a bad day because you did not pray?
7. What hinders you from being God-reliant over self-reliant regarding your prayer life?
8. How are you doing with these four types of prayers: Wow, Help, Thanks, and Please? How do you need to change?

10

Work to Rest

Living a life honoring God requires a person to rest well. If you rest well, you will work well, and the other parts of your life will be satisfying, too. I suspect that most people in first-world countries do not have good rest habits and are unaware or unconcerned about the adverse effects of not resting well. So important is rest that without a sound theology and practice of rest, your work diminishes, and your relationships suffer. What is your theology of rest? How do work and rest intersect symmetrically, making you whole?

Work Hard – Play Hard

If you work without rest, you will burn out. If you rest without work, you will become slothful. Working and resting well make a person productive, wise, and worth emulating. It is a beautiful dichotomy of wholeness—two components that lead to a contented life. The automobile industry illustrates this dynamic duo of work and rest. You have probably heard that it's not wise to buy a car that someone built on a Monday or Friday, though I'm unsure how you would know when your car came down the production line.

The theory suggests that if a person builds a car on those two days, they are either recovering from the past weekend or looking to the next one. This cynical take follows the instincts and habits of our society. The culture's view of rest can be summarized by the term "living for the weekend," where the average worker works hard during the week and plays hard on the weekend. The result is dissatisfaction and no enjoyment of work or rest due to a misunderstanding of their interrelatedness and codependency.

Weekend Rest Theology

The residual effect on the restless soul is incremental discontentment that motivates him to try harder to find fulfillment elsewhere, a pursuit that will never satisfy. He may go to inexhaustible lengths to fill the God-shaped void in his life. This "weekend theology of rest" is the religion of hedonism. In this view, work becomes the necessary evil that finances self-seeking weekend pleasure. Work is the means to the end rather than a part of a worldview that moves toward enjoying and glorifying God in all things (Matthew 6:33; 1 Corinthians 10:31). This worldly work hard, play hard hermeneutic is a disjointed view of life that spawns perpetual dysfunction. There is an ingrownness to this kind of thinking that uses people, places, and things for self-seeking benefits.

- What is your theology of rest? When discussing rest, do you include working rigorously in your discussion?
- Are you a restful person? I'm not merely speaking of time away from work. Is your soul at rest while at work?
- Do you pursue biblical rest that does not live for the weekend but a rest that incorporates work as part of your theology of rest?

To Rest Is to Reflect

I heard a statistic about a group of ninety-plus-year-old people that astounded me so much that what they said drives my philosophy of work, productivity, and spreading God's fame. The question posed to them was, "What would you do differently if you could live your lives over?" Out of the scores of folks surveyed, there were three top answers. I'm unaware of the priority of the order, but here are their responses.

- If I could live my life over again, I would take more risks.
- If I could live my life over again, I would do things of value.
- If I could live my life over again, I would reflect more.

Their last point about reflection is one of the most essential strategies for the restful soul. Our society seems opposed to the notion of reflective thinking. We live too frenetically. The pace of life moves at the speed of the internet. We have reduced our correspondence to tweets, blurbs, and quotes. Stopping, thinking, and reflecting are anomalies in our fast-paced culture (James 1:19). We have too much to do to slow down and contemplate our actions. Reflection is not valued because we do not know how to do it and refuse to take the time to think about it.

The Thinker

Five hundred years ago, we had thinkers. It was a job description. Imagine two kids talking to each other five centuries back about what their fathers did for a living.

Kid #1 – "Hey, what does your daddy do for a living?"
Kid #2 – "My dad is a thinker."
Kid #1 – "Cool. So is mine. I want to be a thinker when I grow up, too."

Thinkers are a thing of the past. The doers have replaced the cautious, deliberate, and introspective. The doer gets things done, though you could make an argument for a lack of quality control (Genesis 2:2). Too many need to learn the true purpose of resting. Resting is not the cessation of work, as though you are kicking your brain in neutral and doing nothing. The Lord rested, but He did not disengage Himself from who He was and what He was doing. He worked while He was resting. Some people see rest as the antithesis of work rather than a component of the work-rest construct. They are not unrelated opposites but coexisting interrelated necessities.

The Vicious Cycle

Those who do not understand this perspective will come home from work and check out of life. His goal will be to do something that does not require his mind, a common and critical mistake. He will likely want to entertain himself with his preferred amusement, a word that means "without the mind." To muse is to think. Amuse is to not think. When the man comes home to amuse himself, he is not relaxing, though it may feel that way. It is like a drug addict taking a meth trip to find relief from the stress of life. Eventually, the addict comes back to earth, and all his stress is still with him. He may have checked out but was not transformed, rested, or satisfied. Thus, he takes another trip like the restless soul living for the weekend. It's more accurate to say he is an addictive soul, not a restless one. If he is wise and humble, he will realize he has not escaped anything but has entered a vicious cycle that has captured him.

To Rest Is to Reclaim

The worn-down person should think about his life and will make vital adjustments. His job does not allow him to do this. He must reclaim what life has taken from him. Rather than succumbing to life's demands by disengaging, he needs a new strategy. Like most tired folks, he thinks that doing nothing is the answer to his stagnation. However, to do nothing is to do something that will never satisfy. To do nothing does not reclaim anything. It fakes out the brain into thinking it is resting when it is not. A wife will talk this way, too. The daily pressures of her responsibilities begin to overcome her. You will hear her say, "I just need a break. A weekend away would be great." Temporarily, she is right, but it won't change what she hopes to change. Like the drug addict, a break would allow her to check out of her responsibilities, but it would not transform her with the fortification she needs to persevere in the duties that await when she returns. Within a day or two of reentering the fray of her life, she will experience exhaustion all over again. She will be ready to take another break, which is not how the Bible teaches us to rest.

Counterintuitive Rest

Let us therefore strive to enter that rest, so that no one may fall by the same sort of disobedience.
(Hebrews 4:11)

The Lord warns us not to stop striving to find rest. Rest requires work; if you work at it, you will discover the sweet spot between work and rest. Because work takes a toll on the soul, you must know how to be proactive about rest. There is a rest for the people of God, but it only comes to the person who works at it. The husband who comes home with a plan to serve his wife will enjoy a restful home. The father, who plans to engage his children, will build a home full of peace. Laziness and disengagement will not bring either of these things. The complaining wife, who lets everyone know how exhausted she is, will not find rest, nor will her family. Her thinking needs to be more in line with God's Word. It's counterintuitive, gospel-informed living. "To work to find rest? How can that be?" You might as well ask, "Will I live if I die?" (See Matthew 16:24-26.) The way of the gospel-centered life is counterintuitive to the typical self-centered person. Let's look at three illustrations about the husband, father, and wife.

The Way to Unrest

- The husband comes home, not considering his wife or how he can serve her. Now multiply that kind of self-centered thinking by ten years. You also have to add all the other times he was self-centered in the marriage. Laziness and selfish habits will not be isolated into one area, i.e., coming home. There will be an all-about-me assault on every sphere of his life, which will exacerbate his familial dysfunction.
- The father who continually checks out of his children's lives will reap a whirlwind of anger and rebellion from them, plus a broken heart. The wrong response is to spend more time at work to escape from his home life. He will become a slave to his career while disengaged and mired in selfishness at home.
- The wife who complains, grumbles, and criticizes will sow seeds of discord and division in her family. The children will walk on eggshells, wondering if they have met her expectations. One teen counselee told me that they would phone ahead to a sibling to see how things were with their mom before coming home. There was no rest in their family.

If these three illustrations are ways to unrest, what is the path to rest?

Working and Resting

When the Israelites crossed the Jordan River, the Lord wanted them to set up memorial stones to remind them of His great work in their lives. He did not want them to forget what He did for them (Joshua 4:1-7). Work should anticipate reflection for redemptive purposes. It reminds me of how I feel after mowing the lawn. I will enjoy a few moments to enjoy my freshly trimmed yard. It brings satisfaction to look over my work and rejoice in the accomplishment. Do you see the interconnectedness of work and rest? The Lord made us for work, not just for the utilitarian purpose of working. Doing a job is more than just getting a task done, whether it is the work you do vocationally or the work you do at home.

To do a job and not enjoy it is detrimental to the soul. The Lord wanted the Israelites to remember and appreciate what He did for them. An aspect of hard work is stopping and reflecting on the good Lord's strength that enables you to do those tasks. Don't be that utilitarian guy who moves from task to task without thinking about all he did, God's fame, or the impact of his work on others. If you don't enjoy His perfected strength in your life, your job will be just that—a job. You will soon exhaust yourself through purposeless grinding. If you work hard at your job and work hard at your home life, you should be able to sit back and rejoice in what God has done through you and the redemptive impact on others.

Resting and Rejoicing

The sequence is that you work, rest, and rejoice. These three things make you complete. Rejoicing in the work done is one way to express gratitude to the Lord. You are acknowledging that He is the one who gives you the power and intelligence to accomplish any task. The person who works hard at work and works hard at rest will be the most restful and grateful because he has experienced God's grace in all areas of his life. He has found the sweet center as work, rest, and rejoicing capture his mind. He understands the interrelatedness and codependency of work, rest, and rejoicing.

He faithfully labors at work and rest and enjoys the Lord's benefits and empowering favor through both of these endeavors. His response is gratitude for God's mercy to him. When a person works hard at work and works hard at rest, there will be fruit that makes the heart glad. If the disengaged husband, father, or nagging wife worked to change, they would find rest for their souls rather than fueling internal discontentment and stirring external chaos. They would have a peaceful home—a grateful one. When the fruit of this type of work-rest ethic materializes, there will be a newfound lifestyle, even while they toil.

Call to Action

1. How much time do you spend in your day or week reflecting on your life? What are the primary means of being reflective, e.g., walking, praying, journaling, talking to others? A good exercise is to slow down and process what you have read here. If you're a busy person, make plans so you can live a more doable pace.

2. Do you work to find rest when you are not at work, or do you try to disengage from life, thinking an escape from doing any work away from work is the solution?

3. Do you work on your time off to bring peace to your home and friends? How have you benefited from proactively planning your time away from work? How have you blessed others by working hard during your rest time?

4. Can you rejoice in the Lord's good work through your efforts on the job, whether it is your vocation, vacation, or your everyday home life? If not, why not?

5. Will you talk to someone about this "working to rest concept," asking them to speak into your life in specific and practical ways? You will benefit most if you allow those who know you best to come alongside you. Plan to do life over coffee with someone and discuss how much work you do to create rest. For example,
   - Do you work to carve out time to reflect daily?
   - Do you work by serving the members of your home, which leads to peace, calmness, and a restful home?

About the Author

Rick Thomas launched the Life Over Coffee global training network in 2008 to bring hope and help for you and others by creating resources that spark conversations for transformation. His primary responsibilities are resource creation and leadership development, which he does through speaking, writing, podcasting, and educating. In 1990 he earned a BA in Theology and, in 1991, a BS in Education. In 1993, he received his ordination into Christian ministry, and in 2000, he graduated with an MA in Counseling from The Master's University. In 2006, he was recognized as a Fellow of the Association of Certified Biblical Counselors (ACBC).

Other Books Available from
Life Over Coffee

Boasting in Weakness
Centering Your Marriage on Christ
Communication
Complete Marriage
Don't Apologize
Exchange the Truth for a Lie
Help My Marriage Has Grown Cold
Identity Crisis
Local Church
Loving Me
Mad
Marriage Devotion We Are One
Politics and Culture
Parenting Devotion from Zero to Adulthood
Sex, Temptation, and Modesty
Storm Hurler
The Cyber Effect
The Talk
Wives Leading
You Decide